The Ultimate
Texas MPJE® Review Guide
2019

Fred S. Brinkley, Jr., R.Ph., M.B.A.
Gary G. Cacciatore, Pharm.D., J.D.

Published by Pharmacy Regulatory Advisors
http://www.txpharmacylaw.com
info@txpharmacylaw.com

March 2019

©2019 Fred S. Brinkley, Jr. and Gary G. Cacciatore. All rights reserved. No part of this publication may be reproduced, stored in a database or retrieval system, or transmitted in any form or by any means electronic, mechanical, photocopying, recording, or otherwise without written permission of the publisher.

VIOLATION OF COPYRIGHT WILL RESULT IN LEGAL ACTION, INCLUDING CIVIL AND CRIMINAL PENALTIES.
The consent of the publisher does not extend to copying for general distribution, for promoting, for creating new works, or for resale. Specific permission must be obtained in writing from Pharmacy Regulatory Advisors.

Trademark Notice: Product or corporate names may be trademarks or registered trademarks and are used only for identification and explanation, without intent to infringe.

978-0-692-19244-3

Table of Contents

- 5   Introduction
- 6   About the Authors
- 7   Acronyms
- 8   Information on the Multistate Pharmacy Jurisprudence Exam (MPJE®)
- 11   MPJE® Competency Statements
- 19   Texas State Board of Pharmacy Candidate's Guide to the Texas Pharmacy Jurisprudence Exam

31   Section One | Federal Food, Drug, and Cosmetic Act (FDCA), Poison Prevention Packaging Act (PPPA), and Other Miscellaneous Federal Laws

- 31   Federal Food, Drug, and Cosmetic Act (FDCA) and Major Amendments
- 34   Prohibited Acts Under the FDCA
- 37   Other Provisions of the FDCA and Federal Regulations
- 43   Poison Prevention Packaging Act (PPPA)
- 45   Other Federal Laws and Regulations
- 48   Privacy – HIPPA, HITECH, and "Texas HIPAA"

53   Section Two | Federal and Texas Controlled Substances Acts

- 53   Drug Classification
- 55   Registration
- 58   Scheduling of Compounded Controlled Substances
- 59   Ordering and Transferring Controlled Substances
- 61   Additional Requirements for Controlled Substances
- 66   Dispensing Controlled Substance Prescriptions
- 70   Schedule II Prescriptions
- 73   Schedule III-V Prescriptions
- 75   Texas Prescription Monitoring Program, Treatment of Opiate Dependence, and Methamphetamine Controls
- 79   Summary of Major Differences Between Texas and Federal Law Related to Controlled Substances

85   Section Three | Texas Dangerous Drug Act (TDDA) and Related Texas Laws and Rules

- 85   Definitions
- 85   Practitioners, Prescriptive Authority, and Valid Prescriptions
- 90   Miscellaneous Provisions in the TDDA

91	Prescribing by Mid-Level Practitioners – Advanced Practice Registered Nurses (APRNs) and Physician Assistants (PAs)
93	Therapeutic Optometrists and Optometric Glaucoma Specialists

97 Section Four | Texas Pharmacy Act (TPA) and Selected Rules

97	Introduction, Definitions, and Texas State Board of Pharmacy
99	Licensing
107	Generic Drug Substitution and Interchangeable Biological Products (Texas Pharmacy Act Chapter 562 Subchapter A and Board of Pharmacy Rule 309)
109	Other Provisions of Texas Pharmacy Act
115	Pharmacy Technicians and Pharmacy Technician Trainees (TPA Chapter 568)
116	Miscellaneous Texas Pharmacy Act Provisions and TSBP Rules

135 Section Five | Complaints, Inspections, Disciplinary Actions, Penalties, and Procedures

135	Notifications to the Public, Complaints, and Inspections
136	Grounds for Discipline
139	Penalties and Procedures

145 Section Six | Class A (Community) Pharmacy Rules

145	Personnel
147	Operational Standards
155	Records

161 Section Seven | Other Classes of Pharmacies

161	Class C (Institutional) Pharmacy Rules
168	Class B (Nuclear) Pharmacy Rules
169	Class D (Clinic) Pharmacy Rules
171	Class E (Nonresident) Pharmacy Rules
172	Class F (Freestanding Emergency Medical Care Facility) Pharmacy Rules
173	Class G (Central Prescription Drug Order or Medication Order Processing) Pharmacy Rules
174	Class H (Limited Prescription Delivery) Pharmacy Rules

177 Section Eight | Compounding Laws and Rules

177	Nonsterile Compounding
179	Sterile Compounding

189 Section Nine | Practice Questions

Introduction

The Ultimate Texas MPJE® Review Guide 2019 is intended to serve as a study guide for the Texas Multistate Pharmacy Jurisprudence Exam (MPJE®) and is best used with the textbook, *Texas and Federal Pharmacy and Drug Law, 11th Edition* with the January 2019 Supplement.

The review guide follows the same general order (with some exceptions) as *Texas and Federal Pharmacy and Drug Law, 11th Edition;* however, the textbook provides more detailed and thorough information on each topic. References to *Texas and Federal Pharmacy and Drug Law, 11th Edition* are indicated in this guide by the abbreviation *TFPDL*.

Texas and Federal Pharmacy and Drug Law, 11th Edition is available for purchase at http://www.txpharmacylaw.com or at Amazon.com.

Study Tips are provided throughout this book to note important material and clarify information that we have found is often misunderstood or causes confusion.

As you experienced when you were a pharmacy student, recent graduate, or a seasoned pharmacist who last sat for an exam more than a few years ago, your study plan and preparation are critical to your success. The Texas MPJE requires you to fully comprehend state and federal laws, regulations, and a pharmacist's responsibilities.

The Ultimate Texas MPJE® Review Guide 2019 has been developed by pharmacy regulatory experts with education and experience in both law and pharmacy. The review guide is designed to assist you in focusing on the elements of the exam that may appear on the Texas MPJE although the authors have no specific knowledge of questions that are on the exam.

The key to success is to allow adequate time in your study plan to review parts of the law that are least familiar to you. We believe this review guide will help in the process and support your successful exam completion.

The authors would like to thank Debra Smith, Kurt Wehrs, and Laura Lee Daigle for their help in the production of this guide.

MPJE is a registered trademark of the National Association of Boards of Pharmacy

About the Authors

Fred S. Brinkley, Jr., R.Ph., M.B.A.

Fred S. Brinkley, Jr. is a native of San Antonio and resides in Austin, Texas. Mr. Brinkley received a B.S. in pharmacy from The University of Texas at Austin (UT), attended Drake University's Graduate School of Public Administration, and received his M.B.A. from UT Austin.

Mr. Brinkley's career has spanned community pharmacy, the pharmaceutical industry, professional associations, pharmacy education, and public service positions in both Iowa and Texas. In 1976, he accepted an appointment as Executive Director of the Texas State Board of Pharmacy, a position he held for two decades. In 1997, Mr. Brinkley became Vice President of Professional Affairs for Medco Health Solutions and remained in this role until 2009. He currently coordinates and teaches the pharmacy law course at UT Austin College of Pharmacy and practices as a pharmacy regulatory consultant. Mr. Brinkley is also a registered pharmacist in Texas and Iowa.

Gary G. Cacciatore, Pharm.D., J.D.

Gary Cacciatore lives in Houston, Texas and currently serves as Associate Regulatory Counsel and Vice President of Regulatory Affairs for Cardinal Health, Inc., a global healthcare company providing products and services that help hospitals, physician offices, and pharmacies deliver better health care to patients.

Prior to joining Cardinal Health, Dr. Cacciatore was an Assistant Professor at the University of Houston College of Pharmacy and the University of Houston Law Center, where he taught courses in pharmacy law and ethics, drug information, and food and drug law. He currently serves as an Adjunct Professor at the University of Houston College of Pharmacy teaching the pharmacy law course.

Dr. Cacciatore received his Doctor of Pharmacy degree with high honors from the University of Florida College of Pharmacy. He earned his Doctor of Jurisprudence degree with honors from the University of Houston Law Center.

Dr. Cacciatore is admitted to the bar in Texas and is a registered pharmacist in Texas and Florida.

Acronyms

Most acronyms are defined the first time they are used in this book (and often several times), but here is a list of some of the major acronyms used:

ACPE	Accreditation Council for Pharmacy Education
APRN	Advanced Practice Registered Nurse
ASC	Ambulatory Surgical Center
CE	Continuing Education
CEU	Continuing Education Unit
CFR	Code of Federal Regulations
CGMP	Current Good Manufacturing Practices
DEA	Drug Enforcement Administration
DPS	Department of Public Safety (Texas)
DTM	Drug Therapy Management
FCSA	Federal Controlled Substances Act
FDA	Food and Drug Administration
FDCA	Food, Drug, and Cosmetic Act
HIPAA	Health Insurance Portability and Accountability Act
LTCF	Long Term Care Facility
MPJE	Multistate Pharmacy Jurisprudence Exam
NABP	National Association of Boards of Pharmacy
NAPLEX	North American Pharmacist Licensure Exam
NDC	National Drug Code
OTC	Over-the-counter
PA	Physician Assistant
PIC	Pharmacist-in-charge
PMP	Prescription Monitoring Program
PPPA	Poison Prevention Packaging Act
PPI	Patient Package Insert
REMS	Risk Evaluation and Mitigation Strategies
TCSA	Texas Controlled Substances Act
TDDA	Texas Dangerous Drug Act
TDSHS	Texas Department of State Health Services
TFPDL	Texas and Federal Pharmacy and Drug Law, 11th Edition
TPA	Texas Pharmacy Act
TSBP	Texas State Board of Pharmacy
USP	United States Pharmacopeia

Information on the Multistate Pharmacy Jurisprudence Exam (MPJE®)

General Information

Registration Bulletin

Detailed information on the MPJE is available from the National Association of Boards of Pharmacy (NABP) NAPLEX/MPJE Registration bulletin which is available for download at NABP's website. The bulletin contains detailed information on registering for the exam, scheduling testing appointments, fees, identification requirements, security, question types, score results, and most importantly the competency statements (see below). Candidates should download and read the registration bulletin carefully.

Exam Content and Structure

The MPJE is a 120-item computer-based examination that uses adaptive technology. This means the computer adapts the questions you receive based on your previous responses. Of the 120 items on the exam, 100 count toward your score. You are allowed 2 ½ hours to complete the exam. The questions not counting toward your score are being pre-tested; however, you will not know which questions count towards your score and which questions are being pre-tested. Because it is a computer-based examination, you cannot go back and review a question or change an answer once you have confirmed it and moved to the next question. You also cannot skip a question. Since there is a penalty for unanswered questions, you should answer all of the questions.

The exam content and questions are developed by board of pharmacy representatives, practitioners, and educators from around the country who serve as item writers. Each state board of pharmacy approves the questions that are used for its particular state.

You must achieve a score of 75 to pass the exam. This is not 75%, but a scaled score whereby your performance is measured against predetermined minimum abilities. The maximum score is 100.

The MPJE consists of several types of questions including multiple choice, multiple response, and ordered response questions. Examples of each question type are provided below:

Multiple Choice Sample Question

A Texas pharmacist must obtain how many continuing education (CE) hours to renew his or her license in each renewal period?

a. 15 hours
b. 20 hours
c. 30 hours
d. 40 hours

Multiple Response Sample Question

Which are permissible ways for a pharmacist to obtain continuing education? Select all that apply.

___ Completing an ACPE accredited continuing education course
___ Attending a Texas State Board of Pharmacy meeting
___ Auditing a course at a College of Pharmacy
___ Taking an Advanced Cardiac Life Support class

Ordered Response Sample Question

Place the following products in order from the least abuse potential to the greatest abuse potential. (All options must be used.) Left-click the mouse to highlight, drag, and order the answer options.

Unordered Options	**Ordered Response**
Tylenol with Codeine #4	_____
Sudafed	_____
Valium	_____
Vicodin	_____

Federal versus State Law

It is important to understand that **no distinction is made on the exam between federal and state law questions.** You should answer each question in terms of the prevailing laws of the state in which you are seeking licensure, which for purposes of this review guide is Texas. This means that you should not see a question on the exam that starts out with the words, "According to the Federal Controlled Substances Act…" Such a question would not be valid because it is asking you to answer the question based on federal law only. If Texas has a law that is different and stricter than the federal law, that is the law that must be followed and would be the correct answer.

MPJE Competency Statements

Each question on the MPJE is tied to a specific competency statement. You must master a certain number of competencies to pass the exam. It is imperative that you read through the competency statements in the registration bulletin. The Texas State Board of Pharmacy also publishes the *Candidate's Guide to the Texas Pharmacy Jurisprudence Exam* which contains Texas-specific competency objectives. We have reprinted both the MPJE® competency statements and the *Candidate's Guide to the Texas Pharmacy Jurisprudence Exam* on the following pages.

MPJE®
Competency Statements
from the
NAPLEX®/MPJE® Candidate Registration Bulletin

Area 1 | Pharmacy Practice (83%)

1.1   Legal responsibilities of the pharmacist and other pharmacy personnel

1.1.1   Unique legal responsibilities of the pharmacist-in-charge (or equivalent), pharmacists, interns, and pharmacy owners

Responsibilities for inventory, loss and/or theft of prescription drugs, the destruction/disposal of prescription drugs, and the precedence of Local, State, or Federal requirements

1.1.2   Qualifications, scope of duties, and conditions for practice relating to pharmacy technicians and all other non-pharmacist personnel

Personnel ratios, duties, tasks, roles, and functions of non-pharmacist personnel

1.2   Requirements for the acquisition and distribution of pharmaceutical products, including samples

1.2.1   Requirements and record keeping in relation to the ordering, acquiring, and maintenance of all pharmaceutical products and bulk drug substances/excipients

Legitimate suppliers, pedigrees, and the maintenance of acquisition records

1.2.2   Requirements for distributing pharmaceutical products and preparations, including the content and maintenance of distribution records

Legal possession of pharmaceutical products (including drug samples), labeling, packaging, repackaging, compounding, and sales to practitioners

1.3 Legal requirements that must be observed in the issuance of a prescription/drug order

1.3.1 Prescription/order requirements for pharmaceutical products and the limitations on their respective therapeutic uses

Products, preparations, their uses, and limitations applicable to all prescribed orders for both human and veterinary uses

1.3.2 Scope of authority, scope of practice, and valid registration of all practitioners who are authorized under law to prescribe, dispense, or administer pharmaceutical products, including controlled substances

Federal and State registrations, methadone programs, office-based opioid treatment programs, regulations related to retired or deceased prescribers, Internet prescribing, and limits on jurisdictional prescribing

1.3.3 Conditions under which the pharmacist participates in the administration of pharmaceutical products or in the management of patients' drug therapy

Prescriptive authority, collaborative practice, consulting, counseling, medication administration (including immunizations and vaccines), ordering labs, medication therapy management, and disease state management

1.3.4 Requirements for issuing a prescription/order

Content and format for written, telephonic voice transmission, electronic facsimile, computer and Internet, during emergency conditions, and tamper-resistant prescription forms

1.3.5 Requirements for the issuance of controlled substance prescriptions/orders

Content and format for written, telephonic voice transmission, electronic facsimile, computerized and Internet, during emergency conditions, conditions for changing a prescription, time limits for dispensing initial prescriptions/drug orders, and requirements for multiple Schedule II orders

1.3.6 Limits of a practitioner's authority to authorize refills of a pharmaceutical product, including controlled substances

1.4 **Procedures necessary to properly dispense a pharmaceutical product, including controlled substances, pursuant to a prescription/drug order**

1.4.1 Responsibilities for determining whether prescriptions/orders were issued for a legitimate medical purpose and within all applicable legal restrictions

Corresponding responsibility, maximum quantities, restricted distribution systems, red flags/automated alerts, controlled substances, valid patient/prescriber relationship, and due diligence to ensure validity of the order

1.4.2 Requirements for the transfer of existing prescription/order information from one pharmacist to another

1.4.3 Conditions under which a prescription/order may be filled or refilled

Emergency fills or refills, partial dispensing of a controlled substance, disaster or emergency protocol, patient identification, requirement for death with dignity, medical marijuana, and conscience/moral circumstances

1.4.4 Conditions under which prospective drug use review is conducted prior to dispensing

Patient specific therapy and requirements for patient specific documentation

1.4.5 Conditions under which product selection is permitted or mandated

Consent of the patient and/or prescriber, passing-on of cost savings, and appropriate documentation

1.4.6 Requirements for the labeling of pharmaceutical products and preparations dispensed pursuant to a prescription/order

Generic and therapeutic equivalency, formulary use, auxiliary labels, patient package inserts, FDA medication guides, and written drug information

1.4.7 Packaging requirements of pharmaceutical products, preparations, and devices to be dispensed pursuant to a prescription/order

Child-resistant and customized patient medication packaging

1.4.8 Conditions under which a pharmaceutical product, preparation, or device may not be dispensed

Adulteration, misbranding, and dating

1.4.9 Requirements for compounding pharmaceutical products

Environmental controls, release checks and testing, beyond use date (BUD), and initial and ongoing training

1.4.10 Requirements for emergency kits

Supplying, maintenance, access, security, and inventory

1.4.11 Conditions regarding the return and/or reuse of pharmaceutical products, preparations, bulk drug substances/excipients, and devices

Charitable programs, cancer or other repository programs, previously dispensed, and from "will call" areas of pharmacies

1.4.12 Procedures and requirements for systems or processes whereby a non-pharmacist may obtain pharmaceutical products, preparations, bulk drug substances/excipients, and devices

Pyxis (vending), after hour's access, telepharmacies, and secure automated patient drug retrieval centers

1.4.13 Procedures and requirements for establishing and operating central processing and central fill pharmacies

Remote order verification

1.4.14 Requirements for reporting to PMP, accessing information in a PMP, and the maintenance of security and confidentiality of information accessed in PMPs

1.4.15 Requirements when informed consent must be obtained from the patient and/or a duty to warn must be executed

Collaborative practice and investigational drug therapy

- **1.5** **Conditions for making an offer to counsel or counseling appropriate patients, including the requirements for documentation**
- 1.5.1 Requirements to counsel or to make an offer to counsel
- 1.5.2 Required documentation necessary for counseling
- **1.6** **Requirements for the distribution and/or dispensing of non-prescription pharmaceutical products, including controlled substances**
- 1.6.1 Requirements for the labeling of non-prescription pharmaceutical products and devices
- 1.6.2 Requirements for the packaging and repackaging of non-prescription pharmaceutical products and devices
- 1.6.3 Requirements for the distribution and/or dispensing of poisons, restricted, non-prescription pharmaceutical products, and other restricted materials or devices

    Pseudoephedrine, dextromethorphan, emergency contraception, and behind-the-counter products, as appropriate

- **1.7** **Procedures for keeping records of information related to pharmacy practice, pharmaceutical products, and patients, including requirements for protecting patient confidentiality**
- 1.7.1 Requirements pertaining to controlled substance inventories
- 1.7.2 Content, maintenance, storage, and reporting requirements for records required in the operation of a pharmacy

    Prescription filing systems, computer systems and backups, and prescription monitoring programs

- 1.7.3 Requirements for protecting patient confidentiality and confidential health records

    HIPAA requirements and conditions for access and use of information

- **1.8** **Requirements for handling hazardous materials such as described in USP <800>**
- 1.8.1 Requirements for appropriate disposal of hazardous materials

1.8.2 Requirements for training regarding hazardous materials

Reverse distributors, quarantine procedures, comprehensive safety programs, and Material Safety Data Sheets

1.8.3 Environmental controls addressing the proper storage, handling, and disposal of hazardous materials

Ventilation controls, personal protective equipment, work practices, and reporting

1.8.4 Methods for the compounding, dispensing, and administration of hazardous materials

All hazardous materials including sterile and non-sterile compounding

Area 2 | Licensure, Registration, Certification, and Operational Requirements (15%)

2.1 **Qualifications, application procedure, necessary examinations, and internship for licensure, registration, or certification of individuals engaged in the storage, distribution, and/or dispensing of pharmaceutical products (prescription and non-prescription)**

2.1.1 Requirements for special or restricted licenses, registration, authorization, or certificates

Pharmacists, pharmacist preceptors, pharmacy interns, pharmacy technicians, controlled substance registrants, and under specialty pharmacist licenses (Nuclear, Consultant, etc.)

2.1.2 Standards of practice related to the practice of pharmacy

Quality assurance programs (including peer review), changing dosage forms, therapeutic substitution, error reporting, public health reporting requirements (such as notification of potential terrorist event, physical abuse, and treatment for tuberculosis), and issues of conscience and maintaining competency

2.1.3 Requirements for classifications and processes of disciplinary actions that may be taken against a registered, licensed, certified, or permitted individual

2.1.4 Requirements for reporting to and participating in programs addressing the inability of an individual licensed, registered, or certified by the Board to engage in the practice of pharmacy with reasonable skill and safety

Impairment caused by the use of alcohol, drugs, chemicals, or other materials, or mental, physical, or psychological conditions

2.2 Requirements and application procedure for the registration, licensure, certification, or permitting of a practice setting or business entity

2.2.1 Requirements for registration, license, certification, or permitting of a practice setting

In-state pharmacies, out-of-state pharmacies, specialty pharmacies, controlled substance registrants, wholesalers, distributors, manufacturers/repackagers, computer services providers, and internet pharmacies

2.2.2 Requirements for an inspection of a licensed, registered, certified, or permitted practice setting

2.2.3 Requirements for the renewal or reinstatement of a license, registration, certificate, or permit of a practice setting

2.2.4 Classifications and processes of disciplinary actions that may be taken against a registered, licensed, certified, or permitted practice setting

2.3 Operational requirements for a registered, licensed, certified, or permitted practice setting

2.3.1 Requirements for the operation of a pharmacy or practice setting that is not directly related to the dispensing of pharmaceutical products

Issues related to space, equipment, advertising and signage, security (including temporary absences of the pharmacist), policies and procedures, libraries and references (including veterinary), and the display of licenses

2.3.2 Requirements for the possession, storage, and handling of pharmaceutical products, preparations, bulk drug substances/excipients, and devices, including controlled substances

Investigational new drugs, repackaged or resold drugs, sample pharmaceuticals, recalls, and outdated pharmaceutical products

2.3.3 Requirements for delivery of pharmaceutical products, preparations, bulk drug substances/excipients, and devices, including controlled substances

Issues related to identification of the person accepting delivery of a drug, use of the mail, contract delivery, use of couriers, use of pharmacy employees, use of kiosks, secure mail boxes, script centers, use of vacuum tubes, and use of drive-up windows

Area 3 | General Regulatory Processes (2%)

3.1 Application of regulations

3.1.1 Laws and rules that regulate or affect the manufacture, storage, distribution, and dispensing of pharmaceutical products, preparations, bulk drug substances/excipients, and devices (prescription and non-prescription), including controlled substances

Food, Drug, and Cosmetic Act(s) and Regulations, the Controlled Substances Act(s) and Regulations, OBRA 90's Title IV Requirements, Practice Acts and Rules, other statutes and regulations, including, but not limited to dispensing of methadone, child-resistant packaging, tamper resistant packaging, drug paraphernalia, drug samples, pharmacist responsibilities in Medicare-certified skilled-nursing facilities, NDC numbers, and schedules of controlled substances

TEXAS STATE BOARD OF PHARMACY

CANDIDATE'S GUIDE TO THE TEXAS PHARMACY JURISPRUDENCE EXAM

As required by the Texas Pharmacy Act, the Texas State Board of Pharmacy administers a Texas Pharmacy Jurisprudence Exam to candidates for licensure in Texas.

TEXAS PHARMACY JURISPRUDENCE EXAM

The Board uses the services of the National Association of Boards of Pharmacy (NABP), and administers their Multistate Pharmacy Jurisprudence Exam (MPJE). Although the MPJE is developed for use by multiple states, all of the exam questions on the Texas version of the exam are applicable to pharmacy practice in Texas. This exam is a comprehensive exam, which includes questions on both federal and state statutes and rules pertaining to the practice of pharmacy in Texas.

The exam is designed to measure each applicant's knowledge of pharmacy law. Candidates should be aware of conflicting areas between Texas and Federal laws and rules and should answer exam questions on the basis of the more stringent statute or rule. You will be given two and one-half hours to answer 120 multiple choice questions.

Since the exam is a qualifying exam, applicants are not competing against each other for a passing score. An applicant is required to attain a score of no less than 75 on the exam. The score is calculated by first determining the candidate's ability level on the MPJE, and then comparing the candidate's ability level to the predetermined minimum acceptable ability level established for the MPJE. An applicant who passes NAPLEX but fails the Texas Pharmacy Jurisprudence Exam is required to repeat only the Jurisprudence exam. If an applicant passes the Texas Pharmacy Jurisprudence Exam but fails NAPLEX, the applicant may use the passing grade on the Jurisprudence examination for licensure purposes for a period of two years from the date of passing the exam.

Rev. 03/18

Candidate's Jurisprudence Examination Guide

COMPETENCY OBJECTIVES

The MPJE Competency Statements, found in the MPJE Registration Bulletin, serve as the blueprint for the topics covered on the Texas Pharmacy Jurisprudence Examination. The competency objectives contained in this document are a detailed supplement to the MPJE Competency Statements.

The attached list of competency objectives provides a guide to the facts and information that you should be prepared to apply to practical situations. Although the exam is a multiple choice exam, the competency objectives are written in an essay format. Test experts believe that one of the best ways to prepare for an exam is to prepare for an essay exam.

HOW TO OBTAIN COPIES OF LAWS AND REGULATIONS

Information regarding Texas Pharmacy Rules & Laws can be obtained from the Texas State Board of Pharmacy website (www.pharmacy.texas.gov).

The Poison Prevention Packaging Act (summary publication) may be obtained from the U.S. Consumer Product Safety Commission's website (www.cpsc.gov).

The Federal Food, Drug and Cosmetic Act may be obtained from the Food and Drug Administration's website (www.fda.gov).

Please note that the Texas Food, Drug and Cosmetic Act is patterned after and tracks the federal Act very closely. The Texas Food, Drug and Cosmetic Act may be obtained at (http://www.statutes.legis.state.tx.us/).

Candidate's Jurisprudence Examination Guide

TEXAS STATE BOARD OF PHARMACY JURISPRUDENCE EXAM COMPETENCY OBJECTIVES

I. Texas Pharmacy Act

Objectives: The candidate should be prepared to:

1. discuss the purpose of the Board;
2. explain the definitions in the Act;
3. describe the qualifications for membership and the make-up of the Board;
4. explain the rule-making authority of the Board;
5. discuss the responsibilities of the Board;
6. discuss inspections by the Board or its representative;
7. explain unlawful practice of pharmacy;
8. discuss pharmacist-intern registration;
9. discuss the number of times a licensing exam may be retaken;
10. list qualifications for licensing by examination and by reciprocity;
11. describe requirements for display of a pharmacist's license and renewal certificate;
12. discuss renewal of a pharmacist's license;
13. describe the mandatory continuing education requirements for renewing a pharmacist license;
14. describe the procedures and effects of placing a pharmacist license on inactive status;
15. list grounds for discipline of a pharmacist's and pharmacy's license;
16. discuss disciplinary action in a Class E Pharmacy;
17. discuss temporary suspension of a pharmacist's and pharmacy's license;
18. discuss the penalties that may be imposed by the Board and methods for reinstatement of a license;
19. describe the application procedures for licensure and renewal of pharmacy licenses;
20. list and give time limits for the items that must be reported to the Board by a pharmacy and pharmacist;
21. discuss administration and provision of dangerous drugs by practitioners;
22. discuss the unlawful use of the word "Pharmacy" and the title "Registered Pharmacist";
23. discuss the requirements for drug substitution;
24. discuss the requirements for emergency refills;
25. discuss the requirements for release of confidential records; and
26. explain the requirements for operating a remote pharmacy service.

Rev. 03/18

Candidate's Jurisprudence Examination Guide

II. Texas Pharmacy Rules of Procedure

Objectives: The candidate should be prepared to:

1. discuss the items that constitute "unprofessional conduct," "gross immorality," or "fraud, deceit or misrepresentation" in the practice of pharmacy, as grounds for discipline of a pharmacist license;
2. discuss the items that constitute failure to establish and maintain effective controls against diversion of prescription drugs as grounds for discipline of a pharmacy license;
3. describe Board disciplinary procedures against a licensee;
4. discuss the application procedure for reissuance or removal of restrictions on a license;
5. discuss the goals and objectives of internship, the requirements for the Texas colleges of pharmacy internship programs, and the requirements for graduates of out-of-state colleges of pharmacy;
6. explain the extended internship program;
7. discuss the duties that a pharmacist-intern may perform;
8. describe preceptor requirements;
9. discuss examination and reciprocity requirements;
10. explain the requirements for renewal of a pharmacist's license that has expired;
11. describe procedures for change of location, name, ownership, or managing officers of a pharmacy;
12. describe the procedures for closing a pharmacy;
13. discuss the return of dispensed prescription drugs;
14. discuss the requirements for prescription pick-up locations;
15. explain the registration requirements of a pharmacy that uses a pharmacy balance;
16. discuss the terms "failure to engage in the business described in the application for a license" and "ceased to engage in the business described in the application for a license;"
17. describe the responsibilities of the pharmacist-in-charge of a pharmacy that experiences a fire or other disaster;
18. discuss notification of theft or loss of a controlled substance or dangerous drug;
19. discuss the Board's inventory requirements;
20. explain the requirements for, and the differences in, the requirements for personnel, operational standards, and records in a:
    - Class A (Community) Pharmacy;
    - Class A-S (Community Sterile Compounding) Pharmacy;
    - Class B (Nuclear) Pharmacy;

Rev. 03/18

Candidate's Jurisprudence Examination Guide

- Class C (Institutional) Pharmacy;
- Class C (Institutional) Pharmacy Located in a Freestanding Ambulatory Surgical Center;
- Class C-S (Institutional Sterile Compounding) Pharmacy
- Class D (Clinic) Pharmacy;
- Class E (Non-Resident) Pharmacy;
- Class E-S (Non-Resident Sterile Compounding) Pharmacy;
- Class F Pharmacy Located in a Freestanding Emergency Medical Care Facility;
- Class G (Central Prescription Drug or Medication Order Processing) Pharmacy; and
- Class H (Limited Prescription Delivery) Pharmacy.

21. explain the similarities and differences in the requirements for the use of pharmacy technicians and pharmacy technician trainees; their duties, ratios, and training in each class of pharmacy listed in number 20;
22. discuss the responsibilities of the pharmacist-in-charge in each of the classes of pharmacy;
23. discuss the pharmacist's responsibilities for patient counseling and the provision of drug information to patients in Class A pharmacies;
24. discuss the requirements for patient medication records in Class A and Class C pharmacies;
25. discuss drug regimen review requirements in Class A and Class C pharmacies;
26. discuss identification of pharmacy personnel in Class A and Class C pharmacies;
27. describe security requirements for each of the classes of pharmacy;
28. describe the requirements for the temporary absence (off-site and on-site) of a pharmacist in Class A (Community) pharmacies;
29. describe the three-file system for prescriptions that is required in Texas;
30. explain the requirements for written, verbal, and facsimile (FAX) prescriptions;
31. list the requirements for a prescription label;
32. explain the requirements for the use of automation in pharmacies;
33. discuss refill requirements for dangerous drugs and controlled substances;
34. explain the procedures for documenting refill authorization;
35. relate the procedures for telephonic and electronic transfer of prescription information between pharmacies;
36. discuss the requirements for maintaining prescription records in a data processing system;

Candidate's Jurisprudence Examination Guide

37. discuss Schedule II controlled substance official prescription requirements and exceptions to the use of Schedule II controlled substance official prescriptions;
38. discuss the requirements and restrictions for prescriptions issued by practitioners not licensed in Texas;
39. discuss the requirements and restrictions for drug therapy management and for administration of immunizations and vaccinations by a pharmacist under written protocol of a physician;
40. discuss the requirements and restrictions for prescriptions carried out or signed by advanced practice registered nurses and physician assistants;
41. discuss the requirements for a Class A Pharmacy that compounds non-sterile preparations;
42. discuss the requirements for a Class A-S Pharmacy that compounds sterile preparations;
43. describe the requirements of a pharmacy providing centralized prescription dispensing services;
44. describe the requirements for a pharmacy providing central prescription drug or medication order processing;
45. describe the requirements for inpatient records of a hospital or ambulatory surgical center;
46. discuss the absence of pharmacist records in a Class C Pharmacy;
47. discuss the requirements for maintaining records in a data processing system in a Class C Pharmacy;
48. describe the requirements for supplying drugs from the emergency room or radiology department of a hospital;
49. discuss the requirements for dispensing prescriptions to outpatients of a hospital;
50. discuss record requirements for Schedule II controlled substances and floor stock in a Class C Pharmacy;
51. describe the limitations for a Class D Pharmacy drug/device formulary and the petition process for an expanded formulary;
52. explain the requirements for pharmacist supervision in a Class D Pharmacy and the petition process for an alternative visitation schedule;
53. discuss the requirements for Class E pharmacies mailing prescriptions to Texas patients;
54. describe the standards for the provision of pharmacy services through an automated pharmacy system;
55. describe the standards for the provision of pharmacy services through a telepharmacy system;

Candidate's Jurisprudence Examination Guide

56. describe the standards for the provision of pharmacy services through an emergency medication kit;
57. discuss the regulations governing pharmacists;
58. explain the procedures for reporting approved continuing education and the penalties for reporting falsely;
59. discuss the procedures for placing a pharmacist's license on inactive status and for reactivating an inactive license;
60. list the requirements for destruction of dispensed drugs;
61. list the requirements for disposal of stock prescription drugs;
62. discuss the regulations concerning generic substitution;
63. discuss requirements for the use of automation in a pharmacy; and
64. describe how a pharmacist can become Board Certified.

III. Federal and State Controlled Substances Acts and Regulations

Objectives: The candidate should be prepared to:

1. discuss the terms defined in the State and Federal Controlled Substances Acts (CSA);
2. discuss who must register with the Drug Enforcement Administration (DEA);
3. describe types of registration and procedures for registering with DEA;
4. relate the procedures and limitations to distribute controlled substances from one registrant to another without obtaining a second registration;
5. discuss the storage requirements for controlled substances in pharmacies;
6. list all records that must be maintained for acquisition of controlled substances;
7. list all records that must be maintained for dispensing and disposition of controlled substances;
8. describe central recordkeeping requirements and restrictions;
9. discuss the requirements for obtaining, executing, and storing DEA order forms;
10. describe the procedures to follow for a theft or loss of DEA order forms;
11. describe the correct procedures for the return of controlled substances to a supplier;
12. state methods for disposing of expired or contaminated controlled substances;

Candidate's Jurisprudence Examination Guide

13. list the legal requirements of prescriptions for Schedule II, III, IV, and V controlled substances;
14. discuss the specific refill requirements for Schedule II, III, IV, and V controlled substances;
15. discuss emergency refill requirements for Schedule III, IV, and V controlled substances;
16. describe the requirements for partial dispensing of Schedule II and Schedule III, IV, and V controlled substances;
17. describe the procedure for a pharmacist accepting an emergency oral order for a Schedule II controlled substance and the pharmacist's responsibilities;
18. describe the Federal "transfer warning" statement and the requirements for its use;
19. explain the possible implications for knowingly dispensing a forged or altered prescription;
20. discuss the Texas CSA restrictions on the sale of over-the-counter (OTC) Schedule V products;
21. discuss Schedule II controlled substance official prescription requirements and exceptions to the use of Schedule II controlled substance official prescriptions;
22. discuss the criteria used to place a drug product in each of the five schedules;
23. recognize commonly used controlled substances and their schedules;
24. describe procedures for reporting a theft or loss of controlled substances to DEA and DPS;
25. briefly discuss requirements for employee screening;
26. explain the procedures for disposing of the DEA registration certificate and unused order forms upon discontinuance or transfer of business;
27. describe the legal use of methadone;
28. briefly explain the special requirements for a practitioner using methadone to treat addiction;
29. briefly explain the special requirements for a practitioner using Subutex® or Suboxone® to treat addiction;
30. discuss a pharmacist's corresponding responsibility for controlled substance prescription orders;
31. describe requirements regarding whom a practitioner may designate as an agent for the purpose of communicating a practitioner's instructions (prescription) to a pharmacist;
32. discuss the requirements to fill a prescription for a Schedule II controlled substance issued by a practitioner not licensed in Texas; and

Candidate's Jurisprudence Examination Guide

33. discuss the conditions and requirements which allow a pharmacist to dispense a fax prescription for a Schedule II controlled substance.

IV. Federal and State Food, Drug, and Cosmetic Acts

Objectives: The candidate should be prepared to:
1. discuss the terms defined in the State and Federal Law;
2. list conditions causing a drug or device to be deemed adulterated;
3. list the conditions causing a drug or device to be deemed misbranded;
4. state the registration requirements for "Manufacturers" and "Distributors";
5. explain the illegal acts of a pharmacist under the Durham-Humphrey Amendments;
6. describe contents of a manufacturer's label;
7. state the minimum number of years prescriptions must be kept;
8. discuss FDA's recall classification system; and
9. briefly explain the requirements of FDA's Good Manufacturing Practice.

V. Texas Dangerous Drug Act

Objectives: The candidate should be prepared to:
1. discuss the terms defined in the Texas Dangerous Drug Act;
2. list the labeling requirements for dangerous drugs dispensed by a pharmacist and by a practitioner;
3. describe the requirements of refilling a prescription;
4. list the classes of persons who may possess dangerous drugs in the performance of their official duties;
5. discuss the records a pharmacy is required to maintain under the Act;
6. describe the primary enforcing agency and legal proceedings under the Act;
7. explain forgery under the Act; and
8. describe the requirements for designation as an agent of a practitioner for the purpose of communicating a practitioner's instructions (prescription) to a pharmacist.

Candidate's Jurisprudence Examination Guide

VI. Miscellaneous Laws and Regulations Pertaining to Pharmacy Practice

1. Hazardous Substances:

Objectives: The candidate should be prepared to:

- summarize the Poison Prevention Packaging Act of 1970 and a pharmacist's responsibilities under the Act; and
- discuss exceptions to the child-resistant packaging requirements for specific products and patient-specific requests.

2. United States Postal Regulations:

Objectives: The candidate should be prepared to:

- state the U.S. Postal regulations for mailing controlled substances.

3. Texas Optometry Act:

Objectives: The candidate should be prepared to:

- discuss the requirements and limitations for prescribing by therapeutic optometrists. The Texas Optometry Act and rules may be viewed at the following link:

    http://www.tob.state.tx.us

Section One

Federal Food, Drug, and Cosmetic Act (FDCA), Poison Prevention Packaging Act (PPPA), and Other Miscellaneous Federal Laws

Section One

Federal Food, Drug, and Cosmetic Act (FDCA), Poison Prevention Packaging Act (PPPA), and Other Miscellaneous Federal Laws

I. **Federal Food, Drug, and Cosmetic Act (FDCA) and Major Amendments**
   A. Food, Drug, and Cosmetic Act of 1938
      1. Following deaths caused by sulfanilamide elixir in 1937, Congress passed the first legislation that required new drugs to be proven safe prior to marketing.
      2. Established the FDA and is the primary federal law dealing with food, drug, cosmetic, and medical device safety today (with many amendments).
   B. Durham-Humphrey Amendments of 1951
      1. Established two classes of drugs: prescription and over-the-counter (OTC).

> ***Study Tip:*** *You are expected to know those pharmaceutical products that require a prescription. It is particularly important to know that certain products in the same drug class may be either prescription or nonprescription depending on the product or the strength. For example, some insulin products are nonprescription; however, certain other insulin products such as Lantus® and Humalog® are prescription only products. Another example is ibuprofen 400 mg, 600 mg, and 800 mg require a prescription while ibuprofen 200 mg does not.*

      2. Authorized verbal prescriptions and prescription refills.
   C. Kefauver-Harris Amendments of 1962
      1. Required new drugs be proven safe and effective for their claimed use.
      2. Increased safety requirements for drugs and established Good Manufacturing Practices (GMPs) for manufacturing of drugs.
      3. Gave FDA jurisdiction over prescription drug advertising.

D. **Prescription Drug Marketing Act of 1987 (PDMA)**
   1. Bans the re-importation of prescription drugs and insulin products produced in the United States (except by the manufacturer).
   2. Bans the sale, trade, or purchase of prescription drug samples.

   > ***Study Tip:*** *TSBP rules on samples are consistent with federal law and prohibit most pharmacies from selling, purchasing, trading, or possessing prescription drug samples. The only exception is for pharmacies that are owned by a charitable organization or by a city, state, or county government and that are part of a healthcare entity providing care to indigent or low income patients at no or reduced cost. Such samples may only be provided at no charge to patients.*

   3. Mandates the storage, handling, and recordkeeping requirements for prescription drug samples.
   4. Prohibits, with certain exceptions, the resale of prescription drugs purchased by hospitals or healthcare facilities.

E. **The Drug Quality and Security Act (DQSA) of 2013** – These amendments to the FDCA addressed two primary topics: large scale compounding by pharmacies and establishment of a framework for a uniform track and trace system for prescription drugs throughout the supply chain.
   1. Drug Compounding Quality Act (DCQA).
      a. Maintains regulation of traditional compounding with states under Section 503A, but establishes a new Section 503B to the FDCA that allows facilities that are compounding sterile pharmaceuticals to register with the FDA as an "Outsourcing Facility."
      b. Outsourcing Facilities that meet the Act's requirements are exempt from the new drug provisions (FDCA Section 505), adequate directions for use (FDCA Section 502(f)(1)), and drug track and trace provisions (FDCA Section 582).
      c. Outsourcing facilities, often referred to as 503B facilities, are permitted to compound sterile products without receiving patient-specific prescriptions or medication orders. They are primarily regulated by FDA and are subject to FDA's Current Good Manufacturing Practices (CGMPs).

d. Compounding pharmacies that are not registered with FDA as an "outsourcing facility" are often referred to as 503A facilities or 503A pharmacies and may only compound products pursuant to an individual prescription or medication order. They are permitted to do limited anticipatory compounding, are primarily regulated by the states, and are subject to USP Chapter <797> quality standards for sterile compounding.

> *Study Tip:* FDA has issued several guidance documents to implement the Compounding Quality Act that are beyond the scope of this review guide. Detailed information may be found at FDA's website.

2. Drug Supply Chain Security Act (DSCSA) (Track and Trace).
   a. Provides for a uniform national framework for an electronic track and trace system for prescription drugs as they move through the supply chain and sets national standards for states to license drug wholesaler distributors.
   b. Applies to prescription drugs for human use in finished dosage form, but certain products are exempted including blood and blood components, radioactive drugs, imaging drugs, certain intravenous products for fluid replacement, dialysis solutions, medical gases, compounded drugs, medical convenience kits containing drugs, certain combination products, sterile water, and products for irrigation.
   c. Manufacturers are required to provide "Transaction Data" for each product sold, and pharmacies are required to receive transaction data and pass this information along if they further distribute the product.
   d. "Transaction Data" includes Transaction Information, Transaction History, and a Transaction Statement.
      (1) Transaction Information includes the product's name, strength, and dosage form; NDC number; container size and number of containers; date of transaction; and name and address of the person from whom ownership is being transferred and to whom ownership is being transferred.

(2) Transaction History is a paper or electronic statement that includes prior transaction information for each prior transaction back to the manufacturer.
(3) Transaction Statement is a paper or electronic statement by the seller that the seller is authorized (licensed), received the product from an authorized (licensed) person, received the transaction information and transaction history from the prior owner if required, did not knowingly ship a suspect or illegitimate product, has systems and processes to comply with verification requirements, and did not knowingly provide false transaction information.
e. Pharmacies that are "distributing" (distributing is defined as providing a drug to anyone other than the consumer/patient as compared to dispensing, which is providing a drug to the patient/consumer) must have a wholesale distribution license and must pass DSCSA transaction data with that distribution. The only exceptions to having a distribution license and passing transaction data are as follows:
(1) When the distribution is between two entities that are affiliated or under common ownership;
(2) When a dispenser is providing product to another dispenser on a patient specific basis;
(3) When a dispenser is distributing under emergency medical reasons; or
(4) When a dispenser is distributing "minimal quantities" to a licensed practitioner for office use.
f. Other provisions of the DSCSA will be implemented gradually, eventually requiring electronic tracking and tracing of product at the individual package level using a unique product identifier on each package by 2023.

II. **Prohibited Acts Under the FDCA**
Nearly all violations of the FDCA cause the products to be adulterated and/or misbranded. It is important to understand the difference between these two concepts. Although drug manufacturers are more likely to violate the FDCA, actions taken by pharmacists (e.g., a dispensing error) could also cause a product

to be adulterated or misbranded. It is likely these are the types of situations that may be covered on the MPJE.
A. Adulteration – A drug is adulterated if:
   1. It contains any filthy, putrid, or decomposed substance.
   2. It has been prepared or held under unsanitary conditions where it may have been contaminated.
   3. The methods of manufacture do not conform to current good manufacturing practices (CGMPs).
   4. The container is composed of any poisonous or deleterious substance which may contaminate the drug.
   5. It contains an unsafe color additive.
   6. It purports to be a drug in an official compendium and its strength differs from or its quality or purity falls below the compendium standard, unless the difference is clearly stated on the label.
   7. It is not in a compendium, and its strength differs from or its quality falls below what it represents.
   8. It is mixed or packed with any substance which reduces its strength or quality or the drug has been substituted in whole or in part.

Study Tip: If a product's strength is less than what is represented on its label, it could be both misbranded and adulterated.

B. Misbranding – A drug is misbranded if:
   1. The labeling is false or misleading in any particular way.
   2. It is a prescription drug and the manufacturer's labeling fails to contain the following information:
      a. The name and address of the manufacturer, packer, or distributor.
      b. Brand and/or generic name of the drug or drug product.
      c. The net quantity (weight, quantity, or dosage units).
      d. The weight of active ingredient per dosage unit.
      e. The federal legend, "Rx only."
      f. If not taken orally, the specific routes of administration (e.g., for IM injection).
      g. Special storage instructions, if appropriate.
      h. Manufacturer's control number (lot number).
      i. Expiration date.
      j. Adequate information for use (package insert and medication guide or patient package insert if required).

> ***Study Tip:*** *These labeling requirements are for the manufacturer's container. When a pharmacist dispenses a drug to a patient pursuant to a valid prescription, the label does not have to contain all of these elements. State prescription labeling requirements would dictate what is required on the label.*

3. It is an OTC drug and fails to contain the following:
   a. A principal display panel, including a statement of identity of the product.
   b. The name and address of the manufacturer, packer, or distributor.
   c. Net quantity of contents.
   d. Cautions and warnings needed to protect user.
   e. Adequate directions for safe and effective use (for layperson).
   f. Content and format of OTC product labeling in "Drug Facts" panel format including:
      (1) Active Ingredients.
      (2) Purpose.
      (3) Use(s) – indications.
      (4) Warnings.
      (5) Directions.
      (6) Other Information.
      (7) ==Inactive Ingredients (in alphabetical order).==
      (8) Questions? (optional) followed by telephone number.
4. It is a drug liable to deterioration unless it is packaged or labeled accordingly.
5. The container is made, formed, or filled as to be misleading.
6. The drug is an exact imitation of another drug or offered for sale under the name of another drug.
7. It is dangerous to health when used in the dosage or manner suggested in the labeling.
8. It is packaged or labeled in violation of the Poison Prevention Packaging Act.

> ***Study Tip:*** *Pharmacists don't usually concern themselves with these labeling requirements as it is expected that manufacturers will label their products appropriately, but you should know the labeling requirements for OTC drugs.*

III. Other Provisions of the FDCA and Federal Regulations
A. Special Warning Requirements for OTC Products in the FDCA

> ***Study Tip:*** *These are special labeling requirements under federal regulations for products containing these ingredients. Normally the manufacturer's label would include these warnings, but you should be familiar with these requirements.*

1. FD&C Yellow No. 5 (tartrazine) and No. 6 (21 CFR 201.20) – Must disclose presence and provide warning in "precautions" section of label that may cause allergic reaction in certain susceptible persons.
2. Aspartame (21 CFR 201.21) – Must contain warning in "precautions" section of labeling to the following effect: Phenylketonurics: Contains phenylalanine ___ mg per ___ (dosage unit).
3. Sulfites (21 CFR 201.22) – Prescription drugs containing sulfites (often used as a preservative) must contain an allergy warning in the "warnings" section of the labeling.
4. Mineral Oil (21 CFR 201.302) – Requires warning to only be taken at bedtime and not be used in infants unless under advice of a physician. Label also cannot encourage use during pregnancy.
5. Wintergreen Oil (methyl salicylate) (21 CFR 201.303 and 201.314(g)(1)) – Any drug containing more than 5% methyl salicylate (often used as flavoring agent) must include warning that use other than directed may be dangerous and that article should be kept out of reach of children.
6. Sodium Phosphates (21 CFR 201.307) – Limits the amount of sodium phosphates oral solution to not more than 90 ml per OTC container. Also requires specific warnings.
7. Isoproterenol inhalation preparations (21 CFR 201.305) – Requires warning not to exceed dose prescribed and to contact physician if difficulty in breathing persists.
8. Potassium Salt Preparations for Oral Ingestions (21 CFR 201.306) – Requires warning regarding nonspecific small-bowel lesions consisting of stenosis, with or without ulceration, associated with the administration of enteric-coated thiazides with potassium salts.

9. Ipecac Syrup (21 CFR 201.308)
    a. The following statement (boxed and in red letters) must appear: "For emergency use to cause vomiting in poisoning. Before using, call physician, the poison prevention center, or hospital emergency room immediately for advice."
    b. The following warning must appear: "Warning: Keep out of reach of children. Do not use in unconscious persons."
    c. The dosage of the medication must appear. The usual dosage is 1 tablespoon (15 ml) in individuals over one year of age.
    d. May only be sold in 1 oz. (30 ml) containers.
10. Phenacetin (acetophenetidin) (21 CFR 201.309) – Must contain warning about possible kidney damage when taken in large amounts or for a long period of time.
11. Salicylates (21 CFR 201.314) – Aspirin and other salicylate drugs must have special warnings for use in children including warning regarding Reye's syndrome. Retail containers of 1¼ grain (pediatric) aspirin cannot be sold in containers holding more than 36 tablets.
12. Alcohol Warning (21 CFR 201.322) – Internal analgesics and antipyretics including acetaminophen, aspirin, ibuprofen, naproxen, ketoprofen, etc., are required to have a warning for persons consuming 3 or more alcoholic beverages per day and to consult with a doctor before taking.
13. OTC Pain Relievers (21 CFR 301.326)
    a. Acetaminophen.
        (1) Must have "acetaminophen" prominently displayed.
        (2) Must warn about liver toxicity.
        (3) Must warn not to use with other products containing acetaminophen and to talk to a doctor or pharmacist before taking with warfarin.
    b. Nonsteroidal Anti-inflammatory Drugs (NSAIDs).
        (1) Must include term "NSAID" prominently on label.
        (2) Must contain "stomach bleeding" warning.

B. Additional OTC Requirements
    1. Tamper-Evident Packaging – Manufacturers and packagers of OTC drugs (except dermatological, dentifrice, insulin, or lozenge products) for sale at retail must package products in a tamper-evident package.

2. Repackaging of OTC Products – A pharmacist that repackages OTC products would be subject to CGMP requirements and would have to meet all additional requirements including tamper-evident packaging if offered for sale to the public.
3. When an OTC product is prescribed and filled as a prescription, the OTC labeling requirements do not have to be followed. The prescription drug labeling requirements would apply and would include the prescriber's directions for use. If an OTC drug is filled as a prescription, any instructions for refills would apply as would expiration dates (valid for one year).

C. **FDA Drug and Device Recall Classifications**
   1. Class I – Reasonable probability product will cause either serious adverse effects on health or death.
   2. Class II – May cause temporary or medically reversible adverse effects on health or where probability of serious adverse effects is remote.
   3. Class III – Not likely to cause adverse health consequences.

> *Study Tip:* Technically, FDA does not have the legal authority to order a recall of a drug. They do have that authority for other products such as medical devices. Because FDA can take other action including seizing products, most companies will comply when FDA requests them to recall a drug, and these classifications apply to drugs and medical devices.

D. **Advertising and Promotion of Prescription Drugs**
   1. Prescription drug advertising is regulated by FDA.
   2. Over-the-counter (OTC) drug advertising is regulated by the Federal Trade Commission (FTC).
   3. Advertising of Prescription Drug Prices (including by pharmacists) – The advertising of prescription drug prices is considered reminder advertising under FDA regulations (21 CFR 200.200). However, such advertising is exempt from FDA advertising regulations provided that the following conditions are met:
      a. The only purpose of the advertising is to provide information on price, not information on the drug's safety, efficacy, or indications for use.

  b. The advertising contains the proprietary name of the drug (if any), the generic name of the drug, the drug's strength, the dosage form, and the price charged for a specific quantity of the drug.
  c. The advertising may include other information, such as the availability of professional or other types of services, as long as it is not misleading.
  d. The price stated in the advertising shall include all charges to the consumer; mailing and delivery fees, if any, may be stated separately.
E. **Patient Package Inserts (PPIs)**
 1. Supplied by the manufacturer and written for a layperson.
 2. Required to be given to patients when prescriptions for certain products are dispensed.
 3. Currently required for:
  a. Oral contraceptives (21 CFR 310.501).
  b. Estrogen-containing products (21 CFR 310.515).
 4. Hospitalized or institutionalized patients – A PPI must be provided to a patient prior to the first administration of the drug and every 30 days thereafter.
 5. Failure to provide a PPI for these drugs would cause them to be misbranded.
F. **Medication Guides (MedGuides)**
 1. Similar to PPI program but without requirements for institutionalized patients.
 2. FDA requires Medication Guides for drugs when:
  a. Patient labeling could prevent serious adverse effects.
  b. Product has serious risks relative to benefits.
  c. Patient adherence to directions is crucial.
 3. Medication Guides must be written in a standard format and in language suitable for patients.
 4. Manufacturers must obtain FDA approval before distributing Medication Guides and are responsible for ensuring that a sufficient number of Medication Guides are provided to pharmacies.
 5. There are well over 300 products that now require a Medication Guide. A complete list of drugs and/or biologicals that are required to be dispensed with a Medication Guide can be found at http://www.fda.gov/Drugs/DrugSafety/ucm085729.htm.

G. **Risk Evaluation and Mitigation Strategies (REMS)**
   1. REMS are strategies to manage a known or potential serious risk associated with a drug or biological product. FDA requires a REMS if FDA finds that it is necessary to ensure that the benefits of the drug or biological product outweigh the risks of the product. A REMS can include a Medication Guide, Patient Package Insert, a communication plan, elements to assure safe use, and an implementation system. It must also include a timetable for assessment of the REMS.
   2. Elements to assure safe use may include:
      a. Special training, experience, or certification of healthcare practitioners prescribing the drugs;
      b. Special certification for pharmacies, practitioners, or healthcare settings that dispense the drug;
      c. Dispensing drugs to patients only in certain healthcare settings such as hospitals;
      d. Dispensing drugs to patients with evidence or other documentation of safe use conditions such as laboratory test results;
      e. Monitoring patients using the drug; or
      f. Enrolling each patient using the drug in a registry.
   3. Example of a REMS – Isotretinoin (Accutane) iPLEDGE Program.
      a. Only doctors registered in iPLEDGE can prescribe isotretinoin. Doctors registered with iPLEDGE must agree to assume the responsibility for pregnancy counseling of female patients of childbearing potential. Prescribers must obtain and enter into the iPLEDGE system negative test results for those female patients of childbearing potential prior to prescribing isotretinoin.
      b. Only patients registered in iPLEDGE can be prescribed isotretinoin. In addition to registering with iPLEDGE, patients must comply with a number of key requirements that include completing an informed consent form, obtaining counseling about the risks and requirements for safe use of the drug, and, for women of childbearing potential, complying with required pregnancy testing and use of contraception.

  c. Only pharmacies registered in iPLEDGE can dispense isotretinoin. To register in iPLEDGE, a pharmacy must select a Responsible Site Pharmacist who must obtain iPLEDGE program information and registration materials via the internet (www.ipledgeprogram.com) or telephone (1-866-495-0654) and sign and return the completed registration form. To activate registration, the Responsible Site Pharmacist must access the iPLEDGE program via the internet (www.ipledgeprogram.com) or telephone (1-866-495-0654) and attest to the following points:
   (1) I know the risk and severity of fetal injury/birth defects from isotretinoin.
   (2) I will train all pharmacists on the iPLEDGE program requirements.
   (3) I will comply and seek to ensure that all pharmacists comply with iPLEDGE program requirements.
   (4) I will obtain isotretinoin from iPLEDGE registered wholesalers.
   (5) I will return to the manufacturer (or delegate) any unused product.
   (6) I will not fill isotretinoin for any party other than a qualified patient.
  d. To dispense isotretinoin, pharmacists must obtain authorization from iPLEDGE via the internet (www.ipledgeprogram.com) or telephone (1-866-495-0654) signifying the patient is registered, has received counseling and education, and is not pregnant.
  e. Product is dispensed in blister packages which cannot be broken, and a 30-day supply is the maximum quantity that can be dispensed.
  f. No refills are allowed.

H. National Drug Code (NDC) Number
 1. A unique 10-character number that identifies a particular drug by manufacturer or packager (labeler), product, and package size.
  a. First 4 to 5 digits = labeler.
  b. Next 3 to 4 digits = specific drug.
  c. Last 1 to 2 digits = package size.
 2. NDC numbers facilitate automated processing of drug data by government agencies, third party payers, wholesalers, and manufacturers.

3. While nearly all drug products have an NDC number, an NDC code does not indicate a drug is approved by FDA.
4. FDA has proposed to standardize the NDC format and move to an 11-digit code, but that proposed change has not yet been adopted.
I. FDA Orange Book
   1. Official name is *Approved Drug Products with Therapeutic Equivalence Evaluations.*
   2. The primary source for determining generic equivalency of drugs.
   3. Available at http://www.fda.gov/cder/ob/.
   4. Uses 2-letter coding system to indicate equivalency with first letter being the key:
      a. A = Drug products that the FDA considers to be pharmaceutically equivalent and therapeutically equivalent.
      b. B = Drug products that the FDA considers NOT to be pharmaceutically equivalent and therapeutically equivalent.
   5. Products with no known or suspected bioequivalence issues:
      a. AA – conventional dosage forms.
      b. AN – solutions and powders for aerosolization.
      c. AO – injectable oil solutions.
      d. AP – injectable aqueous solutions.
      e. AT – topical products.
   6. Products with actual or potential bioequivalence problems, but for which adequate scientific evidence has established bioequivalence for those products, are given a rating of AB.
J. FDA Purple Book
   1. Official name is *Lists of Licensed Biological Products with Reference Product Exclusivity and Biosimilarity or Interchangeability Evaluations.*
   2. Lists biological products that are considered biosimilars and provides interchangeabilty evaluations for these products.
   3. Only biological products that have been designated "interchangeable" may be substituted for the original reference product by a pharmacist in Texas.

IV. Poison Prevention Packaging Act of 1970 (PPPA)
   A. Administered by Consumer Product Safety Commission.

B. Requires child-resistant containers for all prescription and certain nonprescription drugs.
C. Exemptions:
   1. Request of patient or physician.

> **Study Tip:** Only the patient can provide a blanket request for all future prescriptions. The prescriber can only request a non-child resistant container on an individual prescription. The request is not required to be in writing, although it is good practice to have it in writing.

   2. Bulk containers not intended for household use.
   3. Drugs distributed to institutionalized patients.
   4. One package size of OTC drugs designed for the elderly.
   5. Specific prescription and nonprescription drug exemptions include:
      a. Oral contraceptives, conjugated estrogens, and northindrone acetate in manufacturer's dispenser package.
      b. Medroxyprogesterone acetate tablets.
      c. Sublingual nitroglycerin and sublingual and chewable isosorbide dinitrate of 10 mg or less.
      d. Aspirin and acetaminophen in effervescent tablets or granules.
      e. Potassium supplements in unit dose packaging.
      f. Sodium fluoride containing not more than 264 mg of sodium fluoride per package.
      g. Anhydrous cholestyramine and colestipol packets.
      h. Erythromycin ethylsuccinate granules for oral suspension and oral suspensions in packages containing not more than 8 g of erythromycin.
      i. Erythromycin ethylsuccinate tablets in packages containing no more than 16 g erythromycin.
      j. Prednisone tablets containing no more than 105 mg per package.
      k. Methylprednisolone tablets containing no more than 84 mg per package.
      l. Mebendazole tablets containing no more than 600 mg per package.
      m. Betamethasone tablets containing no more than 12.6 mg per package.

n. Preparations in aerosol containers intended for inhalation.
o. Pancrelipase preparations.
p. Sucrose preparations in a solution of glycerol and water.
q. Hormone replacement therapy products that rely solely upon the activity of one or more progestogen or estrogen substances.

> **Study Tip:** It is important to know all of the products that are exempt from the Poison Prevention Packaging Act including details as to strengths and dosage forms.

must know

V. Other Federal Laws and Regulations
A. Federal Hazardous Substances Act of 1966
  1. The Consumer Product Safety Commission administers and enforces this act which is intended to protect consumers from hazardous and toxic substances.
  2. Requires the label on the immediate package of a hazardous product and any outer wrapping or container that might cover up the label on the package to have the following information in English:
      a. The name and business address of the manufacturer, packer, distributor, or seller;
      b. The common or usual or chemical name of each hazardous ingredient;
      c. The signal word "Danger" for products that are corrosive, extremely flammable, or highly toxic;
      d. The signal word "Caution" or "Warning" for all other hazardous products;
      e. An affirmative statement of the principal hazard or hazards that the product presents (e.g., "Flammable," "Harmful if Swallowed," "Causes Burns," "Vapor Harmful," etc.);
      f. Precautionary statements telling users what they must do or what actions they must avoid to protect themselves;
      g. Where it is appropriate, instructions for first aid treatment if the product injures someone;

- h. The word "Poison" for a product that is highly toxic, in addition to the signal word "Danger";
- i. If a product requires special care in handling or storage, instructions for consumers to follow to protect themselves; and
- j. The statement "Keep out of the reach of children." If a hazardous product such as a plant does not have a package, it still must have a hang tag that contains the required precautionary information. That information must also be printed in any literature that accompanies the product and that contains instructions for use.

B. Federal Hazard Communication Standard
1. The Occupational and Safety Health Administration (OSHA) administers and enforces this regulation which requires employers (including pharmacies) that deal with hazardous materials to meet the Hazard Communication Standard. *See 29 CFR 1910.1200.*
2. The standard requires chemical manufacturers and importers to classify the hazards of chemicals they produce or import and to prepare appropriate labels and Safety Data Sheets (SDS), which were formerly known as Material Safety Data Sheets (MSDS).
3. Pharmacies are required to have a written Hazard Communication Plan.
4. The plan must include a list of hazardous chemicals in the workplace, must ensure all such products are appropriately labeled and have a Safety Data Sheet, and must include training for all workers on the hazards of chemicals, appropriate protective measures, and where and how to obtain additional information. *Note: Additional details can be found in OSHA's publication "Small Entity Compliance Guide for Employers that Use Hazardous Chemicals."*

C. Centers for Medicare and Medicaid Services (CMS) Requirements
1. Tamper-Resistant Prescriptions – CMS requires that all written prescriptions meet certain tamper-resistant requirements to prevent unauthorized copying and to prevent counterfeiting (with some exceptions).
2. Medication Regimen Reviews – CMS regulations require a consultant pharmacist to perform a Medication Regimen Review for all long term care patients every 30 days. CMS

has proposed a new rule (not yet in effect) to also require a pharmacist review of a patient's chart at least every 6 months and during the monthly drug regimen review when the patient has been prescribed a psychotropic drug, an antibiotic, or any other drug requested to be included in the pharmacist's monthly review.

D. **Delivering Prescriptions by U.S. Mail or Common Carrier**
   1. Delivery by Mail (postal regulations administered by the U.S. Postal Service) – General postal regulations do not allow dangerous substances to be mailed; however, there are exceptions for prescription drugs.
      a. Noncontrolled – Prescriptions containing noncontrolled substances (Dangerous Drugs) may be mailed by a pharmacy to the ultimate user provided that the medications are not alcoholic beverages, poisons, or flammable substances.
      b. Controlled substances may be mailed to patients under the following requirements:
         (1) The prescription container must be labeled in compliance with prescription labeling rules;
         (2) The outer wrapper or container in which the prescription is placed must be free of markings that would indicate the nature of the contents (including the name of the pharmacy as part of the return address on the mailing package as that may alert individuals that drugs may be in the package); and
         (3) No markings of any kind may be placed on the package to indicate the nature of contents.
      c. Controlled substances may be mailed to other DEA registrants (practitioners, other pharmacies, distributors, or drug disposal firms) provided they are placed in a plain outer container or securely overwrapped in plain paper and all recordkeeping requirements are met.
   2. Delivery by Common Carrier – Any prescription drug may be delivered from a pharmacy to a patient by common carrier such as United Parcel Services (UPS) or FedEx. This includes all schedules of controlled substances and dangerous drugs. Common carriers are not subject to postal regulations.

E. Federal Tax-Free Alcohol Regulations
   1. Pharmacies sometimes use 95% ethanol (190 proof) for compounding purposes.
   2. When used for scientific, medicinal, or mechanical purposes or to treat patients, such alcohol is considered "tax free."
   3. The Alcohol and Tobacco Tax and Trade Bureau (TTB) regulates tax-free alcohol with the federal Bureau of Alcohol, Tobacco, Firearms, and Explosives (ATFE). ATFE is responsible for enforcement.
   4. A user permit must be acquired from TTB and specific record-keeping requirements must be met.
   5. Tax-free alcohol cannot be resold or used in any beverage product.

VI. Privacy – HIPAA, HITECH, and "Texas HIPAA"
   A. Most pharmacies are a "covered entity" under HIPAA and must be in compliance with these requirements.
   B. Notice and Acknowledgement
      1. Pharmacies must provide patients with a "Notice of Privacy Practices" and make a good faith effort to obtain a written acknowledgement of receipt of the Notice from the patient.
      2. The Notice must be provided upon first service delivery to the patient.
      3. The HIPAA privacy rule requires mandatory provisions in the Notice.
   C. Use and Disclosure of Protected Health Information (PHI)
      1. Protected Health Information (PHI) is the HIPAA term for patient-identifiable information.
      2. Pharmacies may use and disclose PHI to provide treatment for payment and for healthcare operations without authorization from the patient.
      3. Pharmacies may also use and disclose PHI for certain governmental functions without authorization from the patient. This includes uses and disclosures for public health activities such as reporting adverse events to FDA, to health oversight agencies such as boards of pharmacies or state drug monitoring programs, and to law enforcement agencies.
      4. Other uses and disclosures, such as for marketing purposes, require a signed authorization from the patient. If the

covered entity receives remuneration for the marketing, the authorization form must expressly inform the patient of such.
    5. Face-to-face communications about alternative drugs or health products are considered part of treatment and not marketing.
    6. Refill reminders for a currently prescribed drug (or one that has lapsed for not more than 90 days) are not considered marketing as long as any payment made to the pharmacy in exchange for making the communication is reasonable and related to the pharmacy's cost of making the communication.
D. Business Associates (BAs)
    1. BAs are persons or entities, other than members of a pharmacy's workforce, who perform a function or service on behalf of the pharmacy that requires the use or disclosure of PHI.
    2. Pharmacies are required to enter into business associate contracts with these BAs, which require the BAs to meet many of the same requirements for protecting PHI as a covered entity under HIPAA.
E. Patient Rights and Administrative Requirements
    1. Patients have a right to access and obtain a copy of their PHI. Pharmacies must comply with a request within 30 days, but may extend time by no more than 30 additional days if they notify the individual of the reason for the delay.
    2. Patients have a right to amend their PHI records and request an accounting of disclosures of their PHI made by a pharmacy under certain circumstances. Pharmacies must comply with a request to amend or request for an accounting of disclosures within 60 days, but may extend by no more than 30 additional days if they notify the individual of the reason for the delay.
    3. Pharmacies must establish policies and procedures to protect from accidental or intentional uses and disclosures of PHI through the use of appropriate administrative, technical, and physical safeguards to protect the privacy of PHI.
    4. Pharmacies must train all employees on privacy policies and impose sanctions on employees for any violations of privacy policies.
    5. Pharmacies must designate a Privacy Official who is responsible for development and implementation of HIPAA-related policies and procedures and compliance.

6. Pharmacies must also designate a contact person to receive complaints. This person may also be the Privacy Official.

F. HITECH Act – The HITECH Act amended HIPAA to strengthen many of its provisions. Among other things, the HITECH Act added a breach notification requirement that requires:
   1. Covered Entities, including pharmacies, to notify individuals of a breach of their "unsecured" PHI within 60 calendar days after the breach is discovered.
   2. BAs must report any breaches of unsecured PHI to the covered entity and provide the identities of each affected individual.
   3. A "breach" is defined as unauthorized acquisition, access, use, or disclosure of PHI that compromises its security or privacy. It does not include instances in which there has been an inadvertent disclosure from an authorized individual to another person authorized to access PHI within the same organization. A breach also does not include instances in which the covered entity or BA has a good faith belief that the PHI is not further acquired, accessed, retained, used, or disclosed.
   4. For breaches affecting fewer than 500 individuals, covered entities must maintain a log of these breaches and notify HHS of these breaches annually.
   5. If more than 500 individuals are affected, the Secretary of HHS and prominent local media must be notified in addition to the affected individuals within 60 days after the breach is discovered.

G. Texas "HIPAA" – Texas privacy laws, among other requirements, have a broader definition of a covered entity and more stringent training requirements. *See TFPDL pages A.42-44.* The Texas State Board of Pharmacy also has specific rules on "Confidentiality" and "Patient Access to Confidential Records" that are generally consistent with HIPAA. One difference, however, is that TSBP rules require a pharmacy to respond to a request for confidential records by a patient within 15 days which is stricter than HIPAA's 30-day timeline. *See TSBP Rules 291.27 and 291.28 or TFPDL pages E.18-20.*

Section Two

Federal and Texas Controlled Substances Acts

- Knows drugs brand/generic
- Who sets the schedule DEA c̄ FDA (common/trusts)

Section Two

Federal and Texas Controlled Substances Acts

Note: Throughout this section, unless otherwise noted, requirements listed as part of the FCSA are the same under the TCSA.

I. **Drug Classification**
   A. Schedule I (C-I) Drugs
      1. High potential for abuse and severe potential for dependence (addiction).
      2. No currently accepted medical use in treatment in the U.S.
      3. Lack of accepted information on the safety of their use under medical supervision.
      4. Include opiates and derivatives such as heroin and dihydromorphine; hallucinogens such as marijuana, lysergic acid diethylamide (LSD), peyote, mescaline; and depressants such as methaqualone.
   B. Schedule II (C-II) Drugs
      1. High potential for abuse.
      2. Have currently accepted medical use in treatment in the U.S. or currently accepted medical use with severe restrictions.
      3. Abuse of the drug or other substances may lead to severe physical or psychological dependence (addiction).
      4. Include opium and other narcotics such as morphine, codeine, dihydrocodeine, oxycodone, acetaminophen with hydrocodone (Vicodin®), methadone, meperidine, hydromorphone, fentanyl, and cocaine; stimulants such as amphetamine, methamphetamine, phenmetrazine, and methylphenidate; and depressants such as pentobarbital, secobarbital, amobarbital, glutethimide, and phencyclidine.
   C. Schedule III (C-III) Drugs
      1. Potential for abuse less than Schedule I or II.
      2. Have currently accepted medical use in treatment in the U.S.
      3. Abuse of the drug or other substance may lead to moderate or low physical dependence (addiction) or high psychological dependence (addiction).
      4. Include some narcotic Schedule II drugs, but in combination with another ingredient such as aspirin with codeine

or acetaminophen with codeine (e.g., Tylenol #3). Also includes some nonnarcotic drugs including suppository forms of amobarbital, secobarbital, or pentobarbital; stimulants such as chlorphentermine, phendimetrazine, and benzphetamine; anabolic steroids including testosterone; and ketamine and paregoric.

> **Study Tip:** Note that the suppository forms of amobarbital, secobarbital, and pentobarbital are Schedule III, but other dosage forms are Schedule II.

D. Schedule IV (C-IV) Drugs
 1. Low potential for abuse relative to Schedule III.
 2. Have currently accepted medical use in treatment in the U.S.
 3. Abuse may lead to limited physical or psychological dependence (addiction) relative to Schedule III.
 4. Include narcotics such as dextropropoxyphene and products with not more than 1 mg of difenoxin and not less than 25 micrograms of atropine sulfate per dosage unit; depressants such as alprazolam, chloral hydrate, diazepam, lorazepam, and phenobarbital; stimulants such as diethylpropion and phentermine; and other drugs such as carisoprodol, tramadol, pentazocine, and butorphanol.

E. Schedule V (C-V) Drugs
 1. Low potential for abuse relative to Schedule IV.
 2. Have currently accepted medical use in treatment in the U.S.
 3. Abuse of the drug or other substance may lead to limited physical or psychological dependence (addiction) relative to Schedule IV.
 4. Include cannabidiol oral solution (Epidiolex®), pregabalin (Lyrica®), antitussive products containing codeine, and antidiarrheal products containing opium.

F. Scheduling of Controlled Substances
 1. Federal – U.S. Attorney General, as head of the Department of Justice (which DEA is under), may add, delete, or reschedule substances but must obtain a scientific and medical recommendation from FDA.
 2. State – The Commissioner of the Texas Department of State Health Services may add, delete, or reschedule substances but cannot override actions by the legislature.

II. Registration
   A. General Information
      1. Every person or firm that manufactures, distributes, or dispenses any controlled substances or proposes to engage in any of these activities must register with DEA.
      2. There is no state controlled substance registration in Texas.
      3. Dispensers (pharmacies and practitioners) register every 3 years with DEA.
      4. Practitioner registrations start with the letters "A," "B," or "F" (or "G" for Department of Defense contractors).
      5. The second letter of the prefix will normally be the first letter of the practitioner's last name for individual practitioners or the first letter of a pharmacy's or hospital's name.
   B. Mid-Level Practitioners
      1. Registration begins with letter "M."
      2. May include advanced practice registered nurses and physician assistants if the state allows them to prescribe controlled substances. Other mid-level practitioners may include ambulance services, animal shelters, and veterinary euthanasia technicians.
   C. Activities Requiring Separate Registrations
      1. Manufacturing (C-I – C-V).
      2. Distributing (C-I – C-V).
      3. Dispensing (C-II – C-V) – Includes prescribing and administration by practitioners and dispensing by pharmacies.
      4. Conducting research (C-I).
      5. Conducting research (C-II – C-V).
      6. Conducting narcotic treatment program (C-II – C-V).
      7. Conducting chemical analysis (C-I – C-V).
      8. Importing (C-I – C-V).
      9. Exporting (C-I – C-V).
   D. Verifying a DEA Registration (number)
      1. Step 1 – Add 1st, 3rd, and 5th digits.
      2. Step 2 – Add 2nd, 4th, and 6th digits and multiply sum by 2.
      3. Step 3 – Add the sum of steps 1 and 2, and the last digit of the sum should correspond to the last digit of the DEA number.

4. Example: DEA # AB1234563.
   a. 1+3+5 = 9.
   b. (2+4+6) x 2 = 24.
   c. Total = 33.
E. **Separate registration is required for separate locations.**
   1. Individual practitioners including physicians, who register at one location but practice at other locations in the same state, are not required to register at another site if they only prescribe controlled substances at that site. If they maintain a supply of controlled substances at that site or if the site is in another state, they would have to register at that site.
   2. Each pharmacy must have a separate DEA registration.
F. Application for Registration – DEA Form 224 for dispensers (practitioners and pharmacies)
G. Exemptions (Who does not have to register with DEA)
   1. An agent or employee of any registered manufacturer, distributor, or dispenser if acting in the usual course of business or employment.

Study Tip: Exempted persons would include pharmacists working in a pharmacy and nurses working in a hospital or physician's office.

2. A common or contract carrier or warehouseman or an employee thereof whose possession is in the usual course of business or employment.
3. An ultimate user (patient) who possesses such substance for a lawful purpose.
4. Officials of the U.S. Armed Services, Public Health Service, or Bureau of Prisons acting in the course of their official duties.

Study Tip: In Texas, these "federal" practitioners can't write Schedule II prescriptions to be filled off base or out of the facility where they practice because they would not be written on a Texas official prescription form. TSBP only issues official prescription forms to DEA registered practitioners. Prescriptions for Schedule III-V controlled substances from these practitioners can be filled off base.

[Handwritten notes at top: "fill under hospital DEA, hosp includes suffix to ID physician"]

H. **Practitioner's Use of Hospital DEA Number**
   1. Interns, residents, staff physicians, and mid-level practitioners who are agents or employees of a hospital or other institution may administer, dispense, or prescribe controlled substances under the registration of the hospital or other institution when acting in the usual course of business or employment.
   2. The hospital must assign a specific internal code for each practitioner authorized to use the hospital's DEA number, and this must be available at all times to other registrants and law enforcement agencies. This internal code shall be a suffix to the hospital's DEA number (e.g., AP1234563-10 or AP1234563-A12).

I. **Temporary Use of Registration Upon Sale of a Pharmacy**
   If the new owner has not yet obtained a DEA registration, DEA permits the new owner to continue the business of the pharmacy under the previous owner's registration provided the following requirements are met:
   1. The new owner must expeditiously apply for an appropriate DEA registration and state licensure.
   2. The previous owner grants a Power of Attorney to the new owner that provides for the following:
      a. The previous owner agrees to allow the controlled substance activities of the pharmacy to be carried out under his or her DEA registration;
      b. The previous owner agrees to allow the new owner to carry out the controlled substance activities of the pharmacy, including the ordering of controlled substances, as an agent of the previous owner;
      c. The previous owner acknowledges, as the registrant, that he or she will be held accountable for any violations of controlled substance laws which may occur; and
      d. The previous owner agrees that the controlled substance activities of the pharmacy may be carried out under his or her DEA registration and shall remain in effect for no more than 45 days after the purchase date.

III. Scheduling of Compounded Controlled Substances

Study Tip: You should know the concentration limits for codeine and opium products and be able to calculate what schedule a particular compounded product would fall in. However, first be sure that the codeine or opium is being compounded with another nonnarcotic therapeutic agent. Any straight narcotic, regardless of concentration, will always be in Schedule II. For example, if codeine or opium is only being mixed with water or simple syrup, it is still a Schedule II regardless of the concentration.

A. A pharmacy may compound narcotic controlled substances pursuant to a prescription as long as the concentration is not greater than 20%. DEA may consider compounding a narcotic prescription greater than 20% to be manufacturing which would require the pharmacy to be registered with DEA as a manufacturer.
B. The narcotic substance must be compounded with one or more nonnarcotic therapeutic ingredients.
C. Concentration limits
   1. Codeine.
      a. C-V limit = 200 mg/100 ml.
      b. C-III limit = 1.8 g/100 ml and 90 mg/dosage unit.

Study Tip: Although concentration limits are the same under Texas law and federal law, Texas requires all codeine and dihydrocodeine products to be dispensed pursuant to a prescription. Products such as Cheracol® and Robitussin AC® are still Schedule V, but they require a prescription. These products contain the maximum amount of codeine allowed for Schedule V. If you add any amount of codeine to these products, they would then be a Schedule III.

   2. Opium.
      a. Federal C-V limit = 100 mg/100 ml.
      b. Texas C-V limit = 50 mg/100 ml.

Study Tip: The Schedule V opium limit under Texas law is 50 mg/100 ml or half the concentration under federal law. This stricter requirement means that most of the commercially available Schedule V products containing opium cannot be purchased without a prescription in Texas. They are Schedule III controlled substances under Texas law and require a prescription.

c. **C-III limit = 500 mg/100 ml and 25 mg/dosage unit.**

> *Study Tip:* A compounded narcotic prescription will never be a Schedule IV.

IV. Ordering and Transferring Controlled Substances
A. Ordering Schedule II Controlled Substances – DEA Form 222
   1. Required for each sale or transfer of C-II drugs (except dispensing to ultimate user).
   2. Each form has three copies (Copy 1 - Brown, Copy 2 - Green, Copy 3 - Blue).
   3. Only one item may be ordered on each numbered line.
   4. Orders for etorphine hydrochloride and diprenorphine must contain only orders for these substances.
   5. The number of lines completed must be noted on the form.
   6. Name and address of supplier from whom the controlled substances are being ordered must be entered.
   7. Must be signed and dated by the person who signed the last application for registration.

> *Study Tip:* This means that only the person at the pharmacy who signed the last application for renewal of the pharmacy's DEA registration is allowed to sign the DEA Form 222 unless that person signs a Power of Attorney authorizing others in the pharmacy to sign.

   8. Purchaser may authorize other individuals to execute forms by creating a Power of Attorney.
   9. Forms that are not complete, legible, properly prepared, or signed will not be accepted.
   10. Forms that show any alteration, erasure, or changes will not be accepted.
   11. Purchaser submits Copy 1 and Copy 2 of the form to the supplier and retains Copy 3.
   12. Supplier records on Copy 1 and Copy 2 the number of containers supplied and the date shipped to the purchaser.
   13. If an order cannot be filled in its entirety, supplier may fill the order in part and supply the balance within 60 days.
   14. Supplier retains Copy 1 and forwards Copy 2 to DEA.
   15. The purchaser records on Copy 3 the number of containers received and the date received.

> **Study Tip:** It is important to understand how each copy of DEA Form 222 is handled and where it is sent. Normally the pharmacy is the purchaser, but in cases where the pharmacy is sending controlled substances to another DEA registrant (such as another pharmacy, a physician, or a reverse distributor), the pharmacy would be acting as the supplier. ==The purchaser always provides DEA Form 222 to the supplier.==

16. If a completed order form is lost or stolen, purchaser must prepare another DEA Form 222 in triplicate along with a statement containing the serial number and date of the lost form and stating that the goods covered by the first order were not received because the form was lost.
17. A pharmacy may fax a completed DEA Form 222 to a supplier in order for the supplier to prepare the order; however, the supplier may not ship the product until the original DEA Form 222 is received and verified.
18. DEA does allow electronic ordering of Schedule II controlled substances through the Controlled Substances Ordering System (CSOS). It allows electronic orders based on digital certificates issued by the DEA Certification Authority. These digital certificates serve as an electronic equivalent to DEA Form 222. All CSOS applications must be audited by an independent third-party auditor prior to use and whenever changes are made to the software to ensure that the software is in compliance with DEA regulations. Use of the electronic ordering is optional; registrants may continue to order using DEA Form 222.

B. Ordering Schedule III-V Controlled Substances
   1. Schedule III-V controlled substances can be ordered through normal ordering processes from a wholesaler or manufacturer but must be documented by a pharmacy with an invoice provided by the wholesaler or manufacturer.
   2. The invoice must contain:
      a. Name of controlled substance.
      b. Dosage form and strength.
      c. Number of units per container (e.g., 100-tablet bottle).
      d. Quantity received (containers).
      e. Date of receipt.
      f. Name, address, and DEA number of registrant from where CS was received.

g. All invoices for controlled substances must be initialed by the receiving pharmacist in Texas (except in Class C-ASC and Class F pharmacies where they must be signed by the person receiving, who does not have to be a pharmacist).

C. Transfers of Controlled Substances – The 5% Rule
   1. A pharmacy does not have to register with DEA as a distributor as long as total quantities of controlled substances distributed during a 12-month period in which the pharmacy is registered do not exceed 5% of the total quantity of all controlled substances dispensed and distributed during that same 12-month period. *(physician initiates the 222 form.)*
   2. Example: A pharmacy dispenses and distributes a total of 10,000 doses (i.e., tablets, capsules, teaspoons, etc.) of all controlled substances (not just CII drugs). This pharmacy would be allowed to transfer 500 doses without being registered as a distributor.
   3. If the transfer is for a Schedule II controlled substance, a DEA Form 222 is required. For Schedule III-V controlled substances, an invoice provided by the supplier is required with all of the required elements as listed in B.2. above.
   4. Transfers can only be made to the address listed on a DEA registration. This applies to all controlled substances, not just Schedule II controlled substances.

> ***Study Tip:*** *Notice that for Schedule II controlled substances, the person receiving the product initiates and fills out the DEA Form 222, which is sent to the supplier or seller. However, for Schedule III-V controlled substances, the invoice is provided by the supplier or seller to the purchaser.*

V. **Additional Requirements for Controlled Substances**
   A. Storage and Security
      1. Pharmacies may store controlled substances in a secure cabinet that is locked.
      2. Pharmacies may store controlled substances by dispersal throughout the noncontrolled stock to deter theft.
      3. Pharmacies may not store all controlled substances on one unsecured shelf.

Study Tip: While many pharmacies keep some or all of their controlled substances in locked storage, it is only required in Texas for Schedule II controlled substances in Class C (institutional) and Class F (Freestanding Emergency Medical Care Facility) pharmacies.

B. Theft or Significant Loss
   1. A theft or significant loss of controlled substances must be reported in writing to DEA within one business day of discovery of the theft or significant loss. DEA also recommends notifying local police.
   2. TSBP also requires notification of a theft or significant loss of controlled substances immediately upon discovery.

Study Tip: Any theft must be reported, but only "significant" losses.

   3. Complete DEA Form 106 (Theft or Loss of Controlled Substances). This form can be filled out online at the DEA's website.
   4. Submitting the DEA Form 106 immediately is not necessary if the pharmacy needs time to investigate the facts, but an initial notification must be provided in writing to DEA within one business day of discovery. If the investigation lasts longer than two months, the pharmacy needs to provide an update to DEA.

C. Miscellaneous DEA Rules and Policies
   1. Convicted Felon Rule – A pharmacy cannot employ someone who has access to controlled substances if the person has been convicted of a felony involving controlled substances unless a waiver is granted by DEA.
   2. Employee Screening Procedures – DEA requires pharmacies to screen potential employees with specific questions regarding criminal history and use of controlled substances.
   3. Employee Responsibility to Report Drug Diversion – Individual employees are required to report any diversion by other employees to a responsible security official of the employer.
   4. Federal Transfer Warning (21 CFR 209.5) – The following warning is required to be on the label of Schedule II-IV controlled substances when dispensed to a patient: "Caution: Federal law prohibits the transfer of this drug to any person other than the patient for whom it was

prescribed." The only exception would be for a controlled substance dispensed in a "blinded" clinical study.

> ***Study Tip:*** *Most pharmacies comply with this requirement by including this language in small print on every prescription label, but it is legally only required for Schedule II-IV controlled substances. It is not required on labels for Schedule V controlled substances or dangerous drugs (noncontrolled substances).*

D. Disposal and Destruction of Controlled Substances
   1. Onsite destruction must be done by submitting to the nearest DEA Diversion Field Office a DEA Form 41 listing the drugs to be destroyed, method of destruction, and at least 2 witnesses. This must be done at least 2 weeks prior to the proposed destruction date. DEA will notify registrant in writing of its decision. Because it is difficult to comply with all other laws including EPA requirements, most pharmacies do not use this method of destruction.
   2. Transfer to an Authorized (Registered) Reverse Distributor – This is the preferred method of destruction and is simply a transfer from one DEA registrant (the pharmacy) to another (the reverse distributor). Because this is a transfer, a DEA Form 41 is not required. The transfer must be documented with an invoice for Schedule III-V controlled substances and a DEA Form 222 for Schedule II controlled substances.

> ***Study Tip:*** *Be sure to understand the difference between use of a DEA Form 41 which is used to destroy controlled substances on the premises of a pharmacy (even though this is rarely done) and transferring controlled substances to a DEA registered reverse distributor for destruction, which requires a DEA Form 222 or an invoice.*

   3. Disposal of Controlled Substances Collected From Ultimate Users and Other Non-Registrants – DEA rules allow pharmacies to modify their DEA registrations to serve as a collector of controlled substances from ultimate users including patients, the personal representative of the patient in the event of the patient's death, and long term care facilities. A pharmacy or hospital is not required to serve as a collector.

4. Disposal of Controlled Substances of a Hospice Patient by Employees of the Hospice – The SUPPORT Act, a comprehensive opioid bill passed by Congress in late 2018, authorizes an employee of a qualified hospice program to handle controlled substances for the purpose of destruction that were lawfully dispensed to a person receiving hospice care. DEA has yet to adopt regulations to implement this law and practice.

E. Inventories
   1. An initial inventory is required on the first day the pharmacy is open for business.
   2. Newly scheduled drugs or drugs moved from one schedule to another must be inventoried on the day scheduled or moved to a new schedule. DEA requires a biennial (every 2 years) inventory that must be maintained in the pharmacy for 2 years. However, TSBP rules require an annual inventory, so pharmacies in Texas must conduct an annual inventory.
   3. Inventory Counts.
      a. An exact count is required for all Schedule IIs.
      b. An estimated count is allowed for Schedule III-V products unless the container holds more than 1000 tablets or capsules.
   4. Although many pharmacies maintain a perpetual inventory of Schedule II controlled substances or even for all controlled substances, a perpetual inventory is only required in Texas for:
      a. Schedule II controlled substances in Class C (Institutional) pharmacies.
      b. All controlled substances stored at a remote location under the remote pharmacy rules.
      c. All controlled substances in Class C Ambulatory Surgical Centers (ASCs).
      d. All controlled substances in Class F (Freestanding Emergency Medical Facility) pharmacies.
   5. TSBP rules require that inventories (other than initial and change of pharmacist-in-charge inventories) be signed by the person(s) taking the inventory and the pharmacist-in-charge and that the signature of the pharmacist-in-charge be notarized within 3 days of the day the inventory is completed, excluding Saturdays, Sundays, and federal holidays.

F. Records
1. Records of controlled substances must be maintained for 2 years under federal and Texas law.
2. DEA requires that records and inventories of Schedule II controlled substances be kept separately from all other records. Records and inventories of Schedule III-V controlled substances must be maintained separately or be "readily retrievable" from other records. "Readily retrievable" means the record is kept or maintained in such a manner that it can be separated out from all other records in a reasonable time or that it is identified by an asterisk, a red line, or some other identifiable manner such that it is easily distinguishable from all other records.
3. Records of Receipt of Controlled Substances.
    a. C-II – Copy 3 of DEA Form 222 (with the number of containers and date received filled in).
    b. C-III – C-V – Supplier's invoice.

> ***Study Tip:*** *TSBP rules require the initials of the receiving pharmacist on invoices for controlled substances except in Class C-ASC and Freestanding Class F pharmacies. In these pharmacies, a pharmacist's initials are not required because there may not be a pharmacist present. Instead, the person receiving all prescription drugs (not just controlled substances) is required to sign for his or her receipt in Class C-ASC and Freestanding Class F pharmacies.*

4. Records of Disbursement of Controlled Substances.
    a. Dispensing records – Although most pharmacies maintain electronic dispensing records, there are still specific storage requirements for the hard copies of all controlled substance prescriptions. TSBP rules require a 3-file storage system:
        (1) File 1 = Schedule II.
        (2) File 2 = Schedule III-V.
        (3) File 3 = Nonscheduled (Dangerous drugs and OTC drugs).

> **Study Tip:** *The 3-file storage system only applies to written prescriptions and verbal prescriptions that are reduced to writing by a pharmacist. If a controlled substance prescription is transmitted electronically, DEA requires that those electronic prescriptions be maintained electronically.*

        b. Other records of disbursement (i.e., controlled substances that leave a pharmacy) include DEA Form 106 (Theft or Significant Loss), DEA Form 41 (Destruction), DEA Form 222 for any Schedule II distributions made under the 5% rule, and invoices for Schedule III-V distributions made under the 5% rule.

  G. Central Recordkeeping
    1. A pharmacy wishing to maintain shipping and financial records at a central location other than the registered location must notify the nearest DEA Diversion Field Office.
    2. Unless the pharmacy is notified by the DEA that permission to keep the central records is denied, the pharmacy may begin maintaining central records 14 days after notifying the DEA.
    3. Central records shall not include executed DEA order forms (Copy 3 of DEA Form 222), prescriptions, or inventories. These must be kept at the pharmacy.

> **Study Tip:** *Be sure to know the records that cannot be kept at a central location.*

VI. Dispensing Controlled Substance Prescriptions
  A. Corresponding Responsibility
    1. For a prescription for a controlled substance to be valid, it must be issued for a legitimate medical purpose by an individual practitioner acting in the usual scope of his or her professional practice.
    2. The responsibility for the proper prescribing and dispensing of a controlled substance is upon the prescribing practitioner, but a corresponding responsibility rests with the pharmacist who fills the prescription. This means a pharmacist cannot simply rely on the fact that a physician has a valid DEA registration to determine if a controlled substance prescription is valid.

3. Through enforcement actions, DEA and TSBP have identified a number of "red flags" that may require a pharmacist to do further investigation as to the legitimacy of controlled substance prescriptions.

> **Study Tip:** You should familiarize yourself with the most common "red flags" and how to resolve them. Common red flags can be found in Chapter B and E of TFPDL and from various sources online such as the TSBP website.

B. Prescriptive Authority
   1. Who can prescribe controlled substance prescriptions is determined by state law. Texas law authorizes the following practitioners to prescribe controlled substances:
      a. Physicians (MD or DO).
      b. Dentists.
      c. Podiatrists.
      d. Veterinarians.
      e. Optometric Glaucoma Specialists (very limited formulary).
      f. Advanced Practice Registered Nurses and Physician Assistants practicing in Texas. In-state advanced practice registered nurses and physician assistants may prescribe controlled substances in Schedules III-V (and in certain practice settings, Schedule II controlled substances) with some restrictions. See Section Three of this Guide.
   2. Designated Agents.
      a. Can communicate a prescription for a C-III – C-V controlled substance but cannot authorize or prescribe.
      b. An authorized agent of the prescriber (employee or non-employee) may not verbally communicate emergency C-II prescriptions to a pharmacist. This task cannot be delegated.
      c. DEA requires that for non-employees of the prescriber to qualify as an agent of the prescriber, there must be a formal written appointment of the agent by the prescriber. This is important for facilities such as nursing homes where the nurses may not be employees of the physician but may wish to call in a prescription to a pharmacy on behalf of a physician.

C. Written Controlled Substance Prescriptions
1. Must be manually signed by the practitioner and dated on the date issued.
2. Must contain:
   a. The full name and address of the patient.
   b. The drug name, strength, and dosage form.
   c. The quantity prescribed.
   d. The name, address, and DEA number of the practitioner.
   e. If written for a Schedule II prescription to be filled at a later date, the earliest date on which a pharmacy may fill a prescription.
   f. Additional requirements for controlled substance prescriptions in Texas:
      (1) The quantity prescribed must be written numerically and as a word. Example: Vicodin #20 (twenty). This is not required for electronic prescriptions. If the quantity is not written as a word, the pharmacist should call to verify the quantity.
      (2) Date of birth or age of the patient.
      (3) The practitioner's telephone number at the practitioner's usual place of business.
      (4) The intended use of the drug unless the practitioner determines the furnishing of this information is not in the best interest of the patient. *(Note: This is required for all prescriptions in Texas, not just for controlled substances.)*
3. Changing Information or Information Omitted.
   a. Schedule II.
      (1) A pharmacist may not change the following items on a Schedule II prescription:
         (a) Name of the patient.
         (b) Name of the drug.
         (c) Name of the prescribing physician.
         (d) Date of the prescription.
      (2) Any other item such as drug strength, dosage form, quantity, or directions for use may be changed provided the pharmacist:
         (a) Contacts the prescribing practitioner and receives verbal permission for the change and

(b) Documents on the prescription that the change was authorized, the name or initials of the individual granting the authorization, and the pharmacist's initials.
  b. Schedule III-V.
    (1) While DEA guidance suggests that a pharmacist may not change the same items (name of the patient, name of the drug, name of the prescribing physician, and date) on a written Schedule III-V controlled prescription, this is not an issue for Schedule III-V prescriptions.
    (2) If a pharmacist needs to change any of those items, the pharmacist can call the prescriber and take a new verbal prescription rather than "changing" the original prescription.
  c. DEA does not allow pharmacists to prepopulate a controlled substance prescription with all required information and then fax or electronically send the prescription to a practitioner to be signed.
D. Verbal, Fax, and Electronic Prescriptions
  1. Verbal prescriptions are not valid for Schedule II controlled substances unless it is an emergency.
  2. Verbal prescriptions are valid for Schedule III-V controlled substances.
  3. Fax prescriptions are valid for Schedule III-V controlled substances but must have the prescriber's original signature. Electronic signatures are not valid on faxed controlled substance prescriptions. Faxes for Schedule II controlled substances are only allowed in limited circumstances. *(See VII. in this Section.)*
  4. Electronic prescriptions for controlled substances (including Schedule II) are valid if both the prescriber's computer and pharmacy's computer meet all DEA security requirements.

Study Tip: *Electronic prescriptions must be from the prescriber's computer to the pharmacy's computer. Faxes are not considered electronic prescriptions.*

VII. Schedule II Prescriptions
A. General
1. Schedule II prescriptions require a written prescription on a Texas Official Prescription Form signed by the practitioner.
2. Verbal prescriptions for Schedule II drugs are not permitted except in an emergency *(see C. Emergency Dispensing of a Verbal Schedule II Prescription below)*.
3. Electronic prescriptions for Schedule II drugs are permitted if all DEA security requirements are met.
4. Schedule II prescriptions cannot be refilled.
5. There is no time limit under federal law as to when a Schedule II prescription must be filled after being issued by the practitioner. However, under Texas law, a prescription for a Schedule II controlled substance must be filled within 21 days after the date issued or the first date authorized to fill.

[margin note: 21 day applies from earliest fill date for multiple scripts.]

> **Study Tip:** *The date issued or the first date authorized to fill would be considered day zero.*

6. Multiple Prescriptions for Schedule II Drugs.
   a. DEA and Texas law permit an individual practitioner to issue multiple Schedule II prescriptions on the same day authorizing the patient to receive a total of no more than a 90-day supply of a Schedule II controlled substance. Instructions indicating the earliest fill date on which the prescriptions can be filled must be on each prescription.

> **Study Tip:** *These prescriptions must be dispensed within 21 days after the earliest fill date indicated. They do not have to be presented to the pharmacy within 21 days after the date issued.*

   b. This 90-day limit only applies when the prescriber is issuing multiple prescriptions for a Schedule II controlled substance on the same day with instructions that some of the prescriptions are not to be filled until a later date. There is no quantity limit on a single controlled substance prescription in Texas. However, insurance plans may limit the amount that may be filled on a single prescription.

> **Study Tip:** The rules for issuing multiple Schedule II prescriptions seem to cause much confusion with pharmacy students and pharmacists. Be sure you understand this concept.

- B. Facsimile Prescriptions for Schedule II Controlled Substances
    1. Facsimiles are generally not valid for Schedule II prescriptions.
    2. However, DEA and Texas law recognize three exceptions where a facsimile can serve as the original written prescription:
        a. A practitioner prescribing a Schedule II narcotic for a patient undergoing home infusion/IV pain therapy;
        b. A practitioner prescribing a Schedule II controlled substance for patients in Long Term Care Facilities (LTCF); and
        c. A practitioner prescribing a Schedule II narcotic for a patient in hospice care.

> **Study Tip:** In Texas, the prescription would need to be a fax of the Texas Official Prescription Form.

- C. Emergency Dispensing of a Schedule II Controlled Substance Pursuant to a Verbal Prescription
    1. In an emergency situation, a practitioner may telephone (or fax) a Schedule II prescription to a pharmacy.

> **Study Tip:** Communication must be from the prescriber and not a designated agent.

    2. Emergency means that the immediate administration of the drug is necessary for the proper treatment of the ultimate user and that no alternative treatment is available and it is not possible for the prescribing practitioner to provide a written prescription.
    3. The quantity prescribed and dispensed must be limited to the amount needed to treat the patient during the emergency period.
    4. The prescription order must be immediately reduced to writing by the pharmacist and contain all information except the practitioner's signature.
    5. If the prescriber is not known to the pharmacist, the pharmacist must make a reasonable effort to determine that the phone authorization came from a valid practitioner.

6. Within 7 days after authorizing an emergency telephone prescription, the prescribing practitioner must furnish the pharmacist a signed written Official Prescription or a valid electronic prescription for the controlled substance prescribed. (If mailed, it must be postmarked within 7 days.) The prescription should be marked, "Authorization for Emergency Dispensing."
7. If the prescriber fails to deliver a written or electronic prescription, the pharmacist must notify the nearest DEA office.

> **Study Tip:** *Remember the quantity that may be prescribed verbally in an emergency is not limited to a specific day's supply (e.g., 48 hours, 72 hours, 7 days). It is the amount needed to treat the patient during the emergency period. The only time limit is the 7 days the prescriber has to send a written Official Prescription or an electronic prescription to the pharmacy.*

D. Partial Dispensing of a Schedule II Controlled Substance Prescription
   1. The Comprehensive Drug Addiction and Recovery Act of 2016 amended the FCSA to allow a Schedule II controlled substance prescription to be partially filled for up to 30 days if requested by the patient or the practitioner who wrote the prescription.
   2. As of the date of this guide's publication, the Texas Controlled Substances Act still requires that any partial filling of a Schedule II controlled substance prescription (except for terminally ill and LTCF patients) be completed within 72 hours. Until the Texas law is amended, it must be followed since it is stricter than the new 30-day time limit under federal law.
   3. For terminally ill and LTCF patients, both federal and Texas law allow partial fills of Schedule II prescriptions as many times as needed as long as the partial fillings are recorded on the prescription or maintained in the pharmacy's computer system. All partial fills for terminally ill and LTCF patients must be completed within 60 days.
E. Official Prescriptions for Schedule II Controlled Substances
   1. Prescriptions for Schedule II controlled substances in Texas must be written on a Texas Official Prescription Form.

2. The Official Prescription Form is issued to prescribers by TSBP and contains security features including:
    a. A unique control number;
    b. A pantograph that reveals the word "VOID" when the form is copied;
    c. Thermochromic ink on the front with the symbol "Rx" that disappears briefly when rubbed; and
    d. A watermark of the Seal of Texas that is visible from either side in regular light.
3. On September 1, 2018, TSBP issued new Official Prescription Forms and notified all users that previous forms, including those issued by TSBP prior to September 1, 2018 and older forms issued by the Texas Department of Public Safety, are invalid and cannot be used effective June 1, 2019.
4. Exemptions to the Use of an Official Prescription Form.
    a. Hospital inpatient medication orders.
    b. Hospital inpatients requiring an emergency quantity of a Schedule II drug upon discharge (limited to a 7-day supply and must be dispensed by the hospital pharmacy).
    c. Persons receiving treatment from life flight helicopter medical team, emergency medical ambulance crew, or paramedic emergency medical technician.
    d. Persons receiving treatment while an inmate in a correctional facility operated by the Texas Department of Criminal Justice.
    e. Animals admitted to animal hospitals or in wildlife parks, exotic game ranches, wildlife management programs, or state or federal research facilities.
    f. Therapeutic optometrists administering topical cocaine as permitted under the Texas Optometry Act.
    g. Prescriptions from out-of-state practitioners, if the pharmacy has a plan approved by TSBP.
    h. Electronic prescriptions.

VIII. Schedule III-V Prescriptions
A. General Rules
    1. May be filled from written or verbal (including facsimile) prescriptions.

2. May be filled from electronic prescriptions as long as all DEA security requirements are met.
3. May be refilled as indicated on the original prescription up to 5 times or 6 months.

> **Study Tip:** There is no limit on the number of partial fills that can be provided so long as the total amount dispensed does not exceed the total number of dosage units authorized and it is within the 6-month time period. Some pharmacy computer systems count each partial fill as a refill and invalidate the prescription after 5 partial fills, but this is not legally accurate. These prescriptions are still valid if the full quantities for all refills authorized have not been dispensed within 6 months.

B. Transfers
   1. Refills of Schedule III-V controlled substances may be transferred to another pharmacy on a one-time basis.
   2. If pharmacies share an electronic, real-time, online database of prescriptions, they may transfer up to the maximum number of refills permitted by law and the prescriber's authorization.
   3. Only refills may be transferred. DEA and TSBP rules do not permit a pharmacy to transfer an original controlled substance prescription that has been received at a pharmacy but not yet filled to another pharmacy. An exception to this is permitted by both DEA and TSBP policy that allows an original electronic prescription for a controlled substance (EPCS), including a Schedule II prescription, to be transferred to another pharmacy if both pharmacies have the capability to forward and receive the EPCS using an electronic sharing program.

   Note: Although the procedure in 3. above is allowed by DEA and TSBP policy, some pharmacies may choose not to follow or allow this policy.

C. OTC Sale of Schedule V Products (exempt narcotics)
   1. The FCSA (and some state laws) allow certain Schedule V products to be purchased from a pharmacy without a prescription.
   2. These are mainly cough suppressant products containing small amounts of codeine such as Robitussin AC and products for diarrhea containing small amounts of opium.

3. While the same laws can be found in the TCSA, because all codeine products require a prescription under Texas law (even Schedule V products) and there are stricter concentration limits for opium products, there are no commercially available Schedule V products that can be purchased without a prescription in Texas. Therefore, these laws are not applicable in Texas.
Note: By policy, TSBP is not enforcing this part of the law since all commercially available Schedule V products in Texas require a prescription.

IX. Texas Prescription Monitoring Program, Treatment of Opiate Dependence, and Methamphetamine Controls
A. Prescription Monitoring Program (PMP)
1. The Texas PMP is administered by the Texas State Board of Pharmacy and collects prescription dispensing data on all Schedule II, III, IV, and V controlled substances dispensed by a pharmacy in Texas or to a Texas resident from an out-of-state pharmacy.
2. The PMP is designed to assist pharmacists and physicians in identifying patients who may be getting prescriptions for controlled substances from multiple physicians or having prescriptions filled by multiple pharmacies.
3. Authorized users of the PMP, including pharmacists and pharmacy technicians acting at the direction of a pharmacist, may access the PMP through the PMP AWARxE portal which can be found at the TSBP website.
4. Users of the PMP may only access the records of their own patients. Unauthorized access of PMP information is a violation of the TCSA, the Texas Pharmacy Act, and TSBP rules.
5. Effective September 1, 2019, practitioners (other than veterinarians) and pharmacists must check the PMP before prescribing or dispensing opioids, benzodiazepines, barbiturates, or carisoprodol. This check is not required if the patient has been diagnosed with cancer or is receiving hospice care and that information is clearly indicated on the prescription.
6. Electronically Transmitting Controlled Substance Prescription Information From the Pharmacy to TSBP.

a. Dispensing information must be transmitted to TSBP no later than the next business day after the date the prescription was filled. If a prescription is partially filled, the information must be transmitted no later than the next business day after the prescription is completely filled.
b. A pharmacy must electronically correct dispensing data submitted to the PMP within seven days of identifying an omission, error, or inaccuracy.
c. The pharmacist is responsible for making sure that the following prescription information is transmitted to TSBP:
    (1) The official prescription control number.
    (2) The prescriber's DEA registration number.
    (3) The patient's (or the animal owner's) name, age (or date of birth), and address (including city, state, and zip code).
    (4) The date the prescription was issued and filled.
    (5) The NDC number of the controlled substance dispensed.
    (6) The quantity of controlled substance dispensed.
    (7) The pharmacy's prescription number.
    (8) The pharmacy's DEA registration number.

Study Tip: *This is the type of information that your pharmacy computer system does automatically, but you are expected to know what information is transmitted and when it is required to be transmitted.*

B. Prescribing and Dispensing of Certain Narcotic Drugs
  1. Methadone is used both for the treatment of severe pain and in the detoxification and maintenance of narcotic addicts in registered narcotic treatment programs.
  2. While any pharmacy can stock methadone, it can only legally be dispensed as an analgesic (for pain treatment).
  3. DEA has requested manufacturers and wholesalers to voluntarily restrict sales of methadone 40 mg to hospitals and narcotic treatment clinics only; no sales to retail pharmacies are allowed.
  4. Methadone (or any other drug) cannot be dispensed for the maintenance or detoxification of addicts unless it is provided through a registered narcotic treatment center.

5. Narcotic treatment facilities may administer and dispense (but not prescribe) narcotic drugs to a narcotic dependent person for detoxification or maintenance treatment.
   a. Short-term detoxification means dispensing of a narcotic drug in decreasing doses for a period not to exceed 30 days.
   b. Long-term detoxification means dispensing of a narcotic drug to a narcotic dependent person in decreasing doses in excess of 30 days but not in excess of 180 days.
6. A physician who is not part of a narcotic treatment program may administer (not prescribe) narcotic drugs (e.g., methadone) to an addicted individual for not more than a 3-day period until the individual can be enrolled in a narcotic treatment program.
7. A hospital that is not part of a narcotic treatment program may administer narcotics to a drug-dependent person for either detoxification or maintenance therapy if the patient is being treated in the hospital for a condition other than the addiction.

C. Office-Based Treatment of Opiate Dependence
   1. The Drug Addiction Treatment Act of 2000 (DATA 2000) allows specially trained practitioners to prescribe certain narcotic Schedule III-V drugs to treat opiate dependence through a risk management program which includes close monitoring of drug distribution channels.
   2. A practitioner authorized to prescribe under the Act, sometimes called a DATA-waived practitioner, is given a DATA 2000 identification or "X" code which must be included with the prescriber's DEA number.
   3. Drugs that may be dispensed under this program are Subutex® (buprenorphine) and Suboxone® (buprenorphine/naloxone combination). These drugs, both Schedule III controlled substances, are available in sublingual form and may be dispensed by a pharmacy upon a prescription from a qualified practitioner.
   4. A DATA-waived physician may be allowed to treat up to 30, 100, or 275 patients, depending on his or her authorization. A DATA-waived APRN or PA may initially treat up to 30 patients. After one year a DATA-waived APRN or PA may apply for authorization to treat up to 100 patients.

5. The Texas Board of Nursing and the Texas Medical Board have agreed that the supervising physician for any DATA-waived APRN or PA that prescribes these products for opioid dependence must also be a DATA-waived physician.

D. The Combat Methamphetamine Epidemic Act of 2005 – This law was passed by Congress to further control the sale of OTC products containing precursor chemicals used in the illicit manufacturing of methamphetamine. The law classifies all products (including multiple ingredient products) containing ephedrine, pseudoephedrine, and phenylpropanolamine as "listed chemical products." Products containing a "listed chemical" are subject to the following requirements:
   1. Display Restrictions – Although the products may be sold by any retailer, covered products must be placed behind a counter (not necessarily a pharmacy counter) or, if located on the selling floor, in a locked cabinet. Texas law specifies that the locked cabinet be within 30 feet and in the direct line of sight of the pharmacy counter.
   2. Retail Sales Limits – Sales of covered products to an individual are limited to 3.6 grams per day and 9 grams per 30 days. Many states have sales limits per transaction.

> *Study Tip:* Texas law has different sales limits, but the federal limits are stricter and must be followed.

   3. Texas law requires the purchaser to be at least 16 years old.
   4. Product Packaging – Covered products (other than liquids including gel caps) must either be in blister or unit-dose packaging.
   5. Logbook Requirements.
      a. Retailer must maintain an electronic or written logbook that identifies the products by name, quantity sold, names and addresses of purchasers, and dates and times of sales.
      b. There is an exception for the logbook requirement for individual sales of a single "convenience" package of less than 60 mg of pseudoephedrine.
      c. Purchaser must present a photo identification issued by a state or federal government, must sign logbook, and enter his or her name, address, and date and time of sale.

            d. Retailer must verify that the name entered in the logbook corresponds to the customer identification.
        6. Employee Training.
            a. Employers certify that employees who deal directly with customers have undergone training to ensure they understand the requirements of the law.
            b. DEA requirements for self-certification and training can be found at www.deadiversion.usdoj.gov/meth/index.html.
            c. Mail Service Limitations.
                (1) Mail service companies must confirm the identity of purchasers.
                (2) Sales are limited to 7.5 grams per 30-day period.
            d. Mobile Retail Vendors ('flea markets").
                (1) Product must be placed in locked cabinet.
                (2) Sales are limited to no more than 7.5 grams of base product per customer per 30 days.

X. **Summary of Major Differences Between Texas and Federal Law Related to Controlled Substances**
    A. Codeine and Opium Products
        1. Codeine-Containing Products.
            a. FCSA – Allows OTC "exempt" sales of Schedule V products containing codeine.
            b. TCSA – Does not allow OTC "exempt" sales of Schedule V products containing codeine. Any codeine-containing product sold in Texas requires a prescription.
        2. Opium-Containing Products.
            a. FCSA – Maximum amount for Schedule V = 100 mg/100 ml.
            b. TCSA – Maximum amount for Schedule V = 50 mg/100 ml.
            c. Any product containing more than 50 mg/100 ml of opium in Texas would be Schedule III or Schedule II (depending on the amount).
    B. Schedule V Controlled Substance Prescriptions
        1. FCSA – Refills not limited to 5 refills/6 months.
        2. TCSA – Refills limited to 5 refills/6 months.
    C. Schedule II Controlled Substances
        1. Special official prescription form required in Texas.
        2. Time limit for filling Schedule II prescriptions.

            a. FCSA – No time limit.
            b. TCSA – 21 days from the date issued or the first date authorized to be filled if multiple prescriptions are issued on the same day with instruction not to fill until a later date.
        3. Partial Fills of Schedule II Controlled Substance Prescriptions.
            a. FCSA – Allows for partial fills for up to 30 days (60 days for LTCF and terminally ill patients).
            b. TCSA – Allows for partial fills for up to 72 hours (60 days for LTCF and terminally ill patients).
    D. Emergency Refills
        1. Schedule III-V.
            a. FCSA – Not addressed.
            b. TCSA and TSBP – Allow emergency refills using pharmacist's professional judgment. *See Section Four, IV.B.*
        2. Schedule II – Not allowed by FCSA or TCSA.
    E. Automatic Refills
        1. FCSA – Not addressed.
        2. TSCA – Not addressed.
        3. TSBP – Allows pharmacies to implement automatic refill programs for controlled substances in Schedules IV and V but not Schedule III. *See Section Four, IV.C.*
    F. Inventories
        1. FCSA – Required biennially (every 2 years).
        2. TCSA – Required biennially (every 2 years).
        3. TSBP – Required annually (every year) and includes a requirement that most inventories be signed by the pharmacist-in-charge and notarized within 3 days of the day the inventory is taken, excluding Saturdays, Sundays, and federal holidays.
        4. Perpetual Inventory Requirements.
            a. Required for Schedule II controlled substances in Class C (Institutional) pharmacies.
            b. Required for all controlled substances in remote pharmacies *(see Board Rule 291.121)*.
            c. Required for all controlled substances in Class C Ambulatory Surgical Centers (ASCs).
            d. Required for all controlled substances in Class F (Freestanding Emergency Medical Facility) pharmacies.

G. Security
 1. FCSA – To deter theft, controlled substances may be stored in a secure cabinet that is locked or by dispersal throughout the noncontrolled drug stock.
 2. TCSA – Same requirements, but TSBP rules specifically require Class C (Institutional), C-S, Class C-Ambulatory Surgical Centers (ASC), and Class F (Freestanding Emergency Medical Facility) pharmacies to have locked storage for Schedule II controlled substances.

H. Records
 1. Prescription Records.
    a. Federal – Three options allowed:
       (1) Two files – One with all controlled substances; one with all noncontrolled substances.
       (2) Two files – One with Schedule II controlled substances; one with all other prescriptions (Schedule III–V and noncontrolled substances).
       (3) Three files as required by TSBP (*see below*).
    b. Texas – TSBP requires three separate files for storage of controlled substance prescriptions; no other options allowed.
       (1) File 1 – Schedule II prescriptions.
       (2) File 2 – Schedule III-V prescriptions.
       (3) File 3 – Dangerous drugs and other noncontrolled prescriptions (OTC).
 2. Invoices – Texas.
    Invoices of controlled substances received by a pharmacy in Texas must have the initials of the pharmacist and actual date of receipt recorded on the invoice. *Note: In Class C Ambulatory Surgical Center (ASC) pharmacies and Class F (Freestanding Emergency Medical Facility) pharmacies, invoices of dangerous drugs and controlled substances must be initialed by the person actually receiving the drug since a pharmacist may not be present to initial the invoice.*

I. Prescription Requirements
 1. Prescription quantity must be written as a figure and spelled as a number in Texas – e.g., #20 (twenty).
 2. Delivered prescriptions must record name of authorized delivery person; person known to pharmacist, intern or delivery person; or address if mailed.
 3. Intended use required on prescriptions in Texas (required on all prescriptions); however, prescriber can opt out.

       4. Name and quantity of drug are required on all prescriptions in Texas.
- J. Methamphetamine Controls
    1. Display Restrictions.
        a. Federal law requires locked cabinet.
        b. Texas law specifies locked cabinet within 30 feet of and in a direct line of sight from a pharmacy counter staffed by an employee of the establishment.
    2. Age.
        a. Federal law – No age requirement.
        b. Texas law – Requires purchaser to be 16 years or older.
    3. Texas law requires nonpharmacy retailers to obtain a Certificate of Authority from the Texas Department of State Health Services.
    4. Texas law requires confirming legality of sale through a real-time electronic logging system.
- K. Inspections
    1. DEA cannot inspect financial, sales, and pricing data without a pharmacist's consent.
    2. TSBP may inspect a pharmacy's financial records in the course of an investigation of a specific complaint without the pharmacist's consent.

Section Three

Texas Dangerous Drug Act (TDDA) and Related Texas Laws and Rules

Section Three

Texas Dangerous Drug Act (TDDA) and Related Texas Laws and Rules

I. **Definitions**
   A. Dangerous Drugs – These include prescription medical devices and prescription drugs that are not controlled substances.
   B. Designated Agent
      1. An authorized person designated by a practitioner to communicate prescription drug orders to a pharmacist.
      2. May be a licensed nurse, physician assistant, pharmacist, or any other individual the practitioner designates.
      3. Practitioner can also authorize a licensed vocational nurse to serve as a designated agent to call in prescriptions for nurse practitioners and physician assistants.
      4. Practitioners must designate in writing each agent authorized to verbally communicate prescriptions, and a pharmacist may request a list of these agents from the practitioner.

> *Study Tip:* A designated agent does not have prescriptive authority and cannot authorize prescriptions. As an agent of the prescriber, he or she is allowed to communicate a prescription to the pharmacist.

II. **Practitioners, Prescriptive Authority, and Valid Prescriptions**
   A. Independent Prescriptive Authority – These practitioners can independently prescribe under their own license.
      1. Physicians (MD and DO).
      2. Dentists (DDS and DMD).
      3. Podiatrists (DPM).
      4. Veterinarians (DVM).
   B. Dependent Authority and Limited Formulary
      1. Physician Assistants (PA) – Dependent authority *(see IV. below)*.
      2. Advanced Practice Registered Nurses (APRN) – Dependent authority *(see IV. below)*.

3. Optometrists – Independent authority but have a limited formulary *(see V. below).*

> ***Study Tip:*** *In certain practice settings, some Texas pharmacists can "sign" prescription drug orders (see Drug Therapy Management Under Protocol in Section Four), but they are not included in the definition of "Practitioner" under the TDDA.*

C. Out-of-State and Canadian/Mexican Practitioners
   1. The Texas definition of "practitioner" includes persons licensed in other states, Canada, and Mexico in a healthcare field who can legally prescribe dangerous drugs under Texas law.
   2. This means that the pharmacist can fill a prescription (written, verbal, or electronic) for a dangerous drug from a physician, dentist, podiatrist, or veterinarian from another state. However, for Canadian and Mexican practitioners, the prescription must be written.
   3. Pharmacists can also fill prescriptions for dangerous drugs from out-of-state advanced practice registered nurses and physician assistants (written, verbal, or electronic), but cannot fill prescriptions for controlled substances from out-of-state advanced practice registered nurses and physician assistants. *(See IV. in this Section.)*
   4. Chart of Valid Prescriptions in Texas *(see next two pages).*

> ***Study Tip:*** *It would be easy to generate questions based on this chart. Be sure you understand which types of prescriptions are valid.*

QUICK REFERENCE GUIDE: PRESCRIPTIONS WHICH MAY BE DISPENSED IN TEXAS

Prescription (Rx) Drug Order Format: / Prescriber Type:	Written Rx (Paper Prescription)	Verbal/ Telephonic Oral/Spoken Rx	Facsimile (Faxed; eFaxed) Rx*	Electronic (Electronic Data File) Rx	Rx may be transferred for initial fill (i.e., Rx is "on hold")	Authorized refills may be transferred between pharmacies	Rx information transmitted (outsourced) to a central fill pharmacy for fulfillment and delivery to patient
DANGEROUS DRUG RX ISSUED BY:							
Texas Physician, Dentist, Veterinarian, Podiatrist, or Therapeutic Optometrists (T&TG)[NOTE]	YES • Manual signature; or • Electronic replica of manual signature printed on secured paper, required.	YES	YES	YES	YES	YES	Centrally filled Rx may be delivered directly to patient or returned to outsourcer pharmacy for delivery to patient.
Authorized Texas Advanced Practice Registered Nurse (APRN) or Texas Physician Assistant (PA)	YES • Manual signature; or • Electronic replica of manual signature printed on secured paper, required; and • Delegating Physician information.	YES Delegating Physician information required.	YES Delegating Physician information required.	YES Delegating Physician information required.	YES	YES	Centrally filled Rx may be delivered directly to patient or returned to outsourcer pharmacy for delivery to patient.
TSBP Authorized Texas Pharmacist Performing Drug Therapy Management (DTM) Under Written Protocol of a Physician	YES • Manual signature; Issued at Hospital, Hospital-based clinic, or Academic health-care Institution • Delegating Physician information	NO	YES • Manual signature; • Issued at Hospital, Hospital-based clinic, or Academic health-care Institution • Delegating Physician information	YES • Issued at Hospital, Hospital-based clinic, or Academic health-care Institution; • Delegating Physician information	YES	YES	Centrally filled Rx may be delivered directly to patient or returned to outsourcer pharmacy for delivery to patient.
Out-of-State[1] Physician, Dentist, Veterinarian, or Podiatrist	YES • Manual signature; or • Electronic replica of manual signature printed on secured paper, required.	YES	YES	YES	YES	YES	Centrally filled Rx may be delivered directly to patient or returned to outsourcer pharmacy for delivery to patient.
Out-of-State[1] Advanced Practice Registered Nurse or Physician Assistant	YES • Manual signature; or • Electronic replica of manual signature printed on secured paper, required; and • Delegating Physician information.	YES Delegating Physician information required.	YES Delegating Physician information required.	YES Delegating Physician information required.	YES	YES	Centrally filled Rx may be delivered directly to patient or returned to outsourcer pharmacy for delivery to patient.
Canadian or Mexican Practitioner	YES • Manual signature; or • Electronic replica of manual signature printed on secured paper, required.	NO Including authorizations for additional refills	NO Including authorizations for additional refills	NO Including authorizations for additional refills	YES	YES	Centrally filled Rx may be delivered directly to patient or returned to outsourcer pharmacy for delivery to patient.

(87)

Copyright © 2019 Fred S. Brinkley, Jr. and Gary G. Cacciatore

QUICK REFERENCE GUIDE: PRESCRIPTIONS WHICH MAY BE DISPENSED IN TEXAS

Prescription (Rx) Drug Order Format: Prescriber Type:	Written Rx (Paper Prescription)	Verbal/ Telephonic Oral/Spoken Rx	Facsimile (Faxed; eFaxed) Rx*	Electronic (Electronic Data File) Rx	Rx may be transferred for initial fill (i.e., Rx is "on hold")	Authorized refills may be transferred between pharmacies	Rx information transmitted (outsourced) to a central fill pharmacy for fulfillment and delivery to patient
CII-V CONTROLLED SUBSTANCE RX ISSUED BY:							
Texas Physician, Dentist, Veterinarian, Podiatrist, or Therapeutic Optometrists (TG)[NOTE]	YES Manual signature required.	YES	YES If a manually signed paper prescription.	YES via application in compliance with DEA rules for EPCS**	NO (Exception**)	YES on a one-time basis (Exception***)	Centrally filled Rx may only be returned to outsourcer pharmacy for delivery to patient.
Authorized Texas Advanced Practice Registerd Nurse (APRN) or Physician Assistant (PA)	YES • Manual signature required; and • for a period not to exceed 90 days; and • Delegating Physician information, including DEA #.	YES • for a period not to exceed 90 days; and • Delegating Physician information, including DEA#.	YES • If a manually signed paper prescription; and • for a period not to exceed 90 days; and • Delegating Physician information, including DEA#.	YES • via application in compliance with DEA rules for EPCS**; and • for a period not to exceed 90 days; and • Delegating Physician information, including DEA#.	NO (Exception**)	YES on a one-time basis (Exception***)	Centrally filled Rx may only be returned to outsourcer pharmacy for delivery to patient.
Out-of-State[1] Physician, Dentist, Veterinarian, or Podiatrist	YES Manual signature required.	YES	YES of a manually signed paper prescription.	YES via application in compliance with DEA rules for EPCS**.	NO (Exception**)	YES on a one-time basis (Exception***)	Centrally filled Rx may only be returned to outsourcer pharmacy for delivery to patient.
Out-of-State[1] APRN or PA	NO	NO	NO	NO	N/A	N/A	N/A
Canadian or Mexican Practitioner	NO	NO	NO	NO	N/A	N/A	N/A
SCHEDULE II CONTROLLED SUBSTANCE PRESCRIPTIONS (CII Rxs):							

• CII Rx may be dispensed only if written on an "official form" provided by the Texas State Board of Pharmacy (TSBP) or if transmitted electronically by a practitioner to a pharmacy in compliance with DEA regulations.**
• CII Rx issued by Out-of-State Practitioners[1] may be filled only by Texas pharmacies that have submitted a plan to TSBP and approved.
• Authorized Texas APRNs/PAs may issue a CII Rx for:
  1) a terminally ill patient who is receiving hospice treatment from a qualified hospice provider; or
  2) a patient hospitalized for 24 hours or greater, provided that the CII Rx is filled at the in-hospital pharmacy; or
  3) a patient receiving emergency services in the hospital's emergency department, provided that the CII Rx is filled at the in-hospital pharmacy.

* **Faxed Rxs** – All must include a statement indicating that the Rx has been faxed (e.g., "Faxed to..."), and name of faxing designated agent, if applicable.
** **EPCS** = Electronic Prescriptions for Controlled Substances (Code of Federal Regulations, Part 1311). CII-CV EPCS may be electronically "forwarded" for initial fill.
*** **Exception** – Pharmacies electronically sharing a real-time, on-line database may transfer up to the maximum refills permitted by law and the prescriber's authorization.
(1) - Includes the United States (other than TX) & U.S. Territories (Puerto Rico, U.S. Virgin Islands, American Samoa, Guam, Northern Mariana Islands).
NOTE: For Rx restrictions for Therapeutic Optometrists (T) & Optometric Glaucoma Specialists (TG), visit: www.pharmacy.texas.gov/files_pdf/Optometrists.pdf

D. Miscellaneous Prescriber Issues
   1. Scope of Practice.
      a. Physician practitioners can legally prescribe drugs to treat any disease or illness in humans even if they have chosen to specialize in a certain type of practice.
      b. For other practitioners, prescriptive authority is limited to their area of practice. This means that a prescription from a dentist must be to treat a dental issue, and a prescription from a podiatrist must be to treat an ailment related to the foot. Similarly, a veterinarian could not prescribe for a human.
      c. APRNs and PAs can prescribe under a prescriptive authority agreement with a supervising physician or under a facility protocol and have limitations on prescribing controlled substances. *See IV. below.*
   2. Self-Prescribing and Prescribing for Family Members.
      a. There is nothing in federal or Texas law that strictly prohibits self-prescribing or prescribing for family members for either dangerous drugs or controlled substances.
      b. However, Texas Medical Board rules state that inappropriate prescribing by physicians includes prescribing dangerous drugs or controlled substances for oneself, family members, or others in which there is a close personal relationship.
      c. The Texas Medical Board does permit prescribing of controlled substances to such individuals to meet immediate needs which is defined as no more than a 72-hour supply.
   3. Prescriptions for "Office Use."
      a. There is no such thing as a prescription for office use.
      b. If prescribers wish to purchase dangerous drugs or controlled substances for their "office use," they should order the drugs from a manufacturer, wholesaler, or pharmacy using an invoice or DEA Form 222 for a Schedule II controlled substance.
   4. What happens to prescriptions with refills when the prescriber dies?
      There are no specific laws or rules regarding this situation.

However, both the Texas State Board of Pharmacy and the Texas Medical Board have agreed by policy that it is an acceptable practice for a pharmacist to provide a 30-day supply of the medication and inform the patient that he or she needs to find a new practitioner.

III. **Miscellaneous Provisions in the TDDA**
    A. Pharmacists cannot possess dangerous drugs unless acting as an agent of a licensed pharmacy (e.g., when delivering a prescription to a patient's home).
    B. Nurses of Home and Community Support Agencies may purchase, store, or transport the following drugs (in a portable sealed container) without being in violation of the Texas Dangerous Drug Act:
       1. Sterile water for injection and irrigation.
       2. Sterile saline for injection and irrigation.
       3. Hepatitis B vaccine.
       4. Influenza vaccine.
       5. Tuberculin purified protein derivative for TB testing.
       6. Not more than 5 dosage units of:
          a. Heparin sodium lock flush – 10 units/ml or 100 units/ml.
          b. Epinephrine 1:1000.
          c. Diphenhydramine 50 mg/ml.
          d. Methylprednisolone 125 mg/2 ml.
          e. Naloxone 1 mg/ml in a 2 ml vial.
          f. Promethazine 25 mg/ml.
          g. Glucagon injection 1 mg/ml.
          h. Furosemide 10 mg/ml.
          i. Lidocaine 2.5% and prilocaine 2.5% in a 5 gm tube.
          j. Lidocaine solution 1% in a 2 ml vial.
    C. Opioid Antagonists *(TSBP Rule 295.14)*
       1. A pharmacist may dispense an opioid antagonist under a valid prescription, including a prescription issued by a standing order, to:
          a. A person at risk of experiencing an opioid-related drug overdose or
          b. A family member, friend, or other person in a position to assist a person at risk of experiencing an opioid-related drug overdose.

2. A prescription dispensed under this section is considered as dispensed for a legitimate medical purpose in the usual course of professional practice.
3. A pharmacist who, acting in good faith and with reasonable care, dispenses or does not dispense an opioid antagonist under a valid prescription is not subject to any criminal or civil liability or any professional disciplinary action for:
   a. Dispensing or failing to dispense the opioid antagonist or
   b. If the pharmacist chooses to dispense an opioid antagonist, any outcome resulting from the eventual administration of the opioid antagonist.

IV. **Prescribing by Mid-Level Practitioners – Advanced Practice Registered Nurses (APRNs) and Physician Assistants (PAs)**
   A. General Requirements
      1. May prescribe under a Prescriptive Authority Agreement with a supervising physician that identifies the locations and types or categories of drugs that may be prescribed.
      2. In a hospital or long term care facility, prescriptive authority may be delegated to APRNs and PAs through a facility protocol. Freestanding clinics or other medical practices owned or operated by a hospital or long term care facility are not considered facility-based practices.
      3. For prescriptions for a child fewer than 2 years of age, the APRN/PA must consult with the delegating physician and the consultation must be noted in the patient's chart.
      4. A physician may not supervise more than 7 APRNs or PAs, except in medically underserved areas or in a facility-based practice in a hospital or long term care facility.
      5. Written prescriptions must contain the name, address, telephone number, and identifying number of the supervising physician, as well as the APRN or PA.

Study Tip: Previously, the prescription label also had to contain the name of the APRN/PA and the name of the supervising physician. The name of the supervising physician is not required. The label is only required to list the prescribing APRN/PA.

B. Controlled Substance Prescribing by Texas APRNS and PAs
   1. Prescribing of Schedule II controlled substances by APRNs and PAs is not generally permitted except in a hospital-based practice under policies approved by the medical staff. Patients must be admitted to the hospital for an intended length of stay of 24 hours or greater or be receiving care in the emergency department or have a terminal illness and are under hospice care.

> *Study Tip:* APRNs and PAs in any practice setting may have prescriptive authority for Schedule III-V controlled substances. Schedule II prescriptive authority is limited to APRNs and PAs in hospital-based practices or for terminally ill patients receiving hospice care from a qualified hospice provider in any setting.

   2. Schedule III, IV, and V prescriptions may be prescribed by an APRN/PA in any practice setting, but the total quantity prescribed, including any refills, may not exceed a 90-day supply.

> *Study Tip:* Remember this 90-day supply limit only applies to APRNs and PAs. A physician or other practitioner with full independent prescriptive authority can prescribe more than a 90-day supply with no limits.

   3. The APRN/PA must be registered with DEA as a mid-level practitioner.
   4. The DEA number of the APRN/PA and the supervising physician must be on the prescription.

> *Study Tip:* Prescriptions from out-of-state APRNs or PAs for controlled substances are not valid in Texas even if these practitioners are registered with DEA and have prescriptive authority for controlled substances in the state where they are licensed.

V. Therapeutic Optometrists and Optometric Glaucoma Specialists
A. **Therapeutic Optometrists (license ends in letter "T")** – Have independent but limited prescriptive authority. They may prescribe:
   1. Ophthalmic devices.
   2. OTC oral medications.
   3. Topical ocular pharmaceutical agents approved by the Optometry Board.
B. Optometric Glaucoma Specialists (license ends in letters "TG") – May prescribe oral medications in the following classifications:
   1. One 10-day supply of oral antibiotics.
   2. One 72-hour supply of oral antihistamines.
   3. One 7-day supply of oral nonsteroidal anti-inflammatories.
   4. One 3-day supply of an analgesic in Schedule III, IV, and V (requires a DEA registration).
   5. Any other oral pharmaceutical agent approved by the Texas Optometry Board and Texas Medical Board (including glaucoma drugs).
C. Glaucoma Restrictions
   1. Must be certified as an optometric glaucoma specialist.
   2. Must consult with an ophthalmologist within 30 days after diagnosing glaucoma.
   3. Before prescribing a beta blocker, must take a complete case history and determine if patient has had a physical exam in the last 180 days.
   4. If no physical exam or the patient has a history of congestive heart failure, bradycardia, heart block, asthma, or COPD, the optometrist must refer patient to an ophthalmologist.
D. Cocaine Eye Drops for Diagnostic Purposes
   1. Therapeutic Optometrists and Optometric Glaucoma Specialists may possess and administer but not dispense no greater than a 10% solution of cocaine eye drops in prepackaged liquid form (solution cannot be compounded).
   2. Must have a DEA registration to possess and store cocaine eye drops and cannot store more than two vials.

DRUGS THAT MAY BE PRESCRIBED BY OPTOMETRISTS

The type of drugs that may be prescribed depends on whether the licensee is an Optometrist, a Therapeutic Optometrist, or an Optometric Glaucoma Specialist.

OPTOMETRISTS (identified by a license number without letters): May not prescribe any prescription drugs.

THERAPEUTIC OPTOMETRISTS (identified by a license number ending in the letter T): May prescribe the appropriate **topical medication** for the purpose of diagnosing and treating visual defects, abnormal conditions, and diseases of the human vision system, including the eye and adnexa (associated anatomic parts). The following is a partial list of topical medications that Therapeutic Optometrists may prescribe.

Therapeutic Class	Type or Mechanism of Action	Generic Name (Partial List)
Anti-Allergy	Antihistamine	Levocabastine HCL, Olopatadine HCL, Pyrilamine Maleate, Lodoxamide Tromethamine, Pheniramine Maleate
	Membrane Stabilizer	Cromolyn Sodium
Anti-Fungal	Imidazoles	
	Polyenes	Natamycin
Anti-Infective	Agents Affecting Intermediary Metabolism	Sodium Sulfacetamide, Sulfisoxazole, Trimethoprim
	Aminoglycoside	Gentamicin, Tobramycin, Neomycin
	Anti-ACHase	
	Anti-Cell Membrane	Gramicidin, Polymyxin B Sulfacte
	Anti-Cell Wall Synthesis	Bacitracin
	Anti-DNA Synthesis	Ciprofloxacin
	Anti-Protein Synthesis (excluding chloramphenicol)	Erythromycin, Oxytetracycline HCL, Mupirocin
	Anti-Viral	Idoxuridine, Tribluridine, Vidarabine
	Cephalosporin	Cefazolin
Anti-Inflammatory	Nonsteroidal Anti-Inflammatory (NSAID)	Diclofenac Sodium, Flurbiprofen Sodium, Ketorolac Tromethamine, Suprofen
	Steroid	Dexamethasone, Hydrocortisone, Prednisolone Acetate, Remixolone, Fluorometholone, Medrysone, Prednisolone Sodium
Antiseptic		Zinc Sulfate
Chelating Agent		Deferoxamine, EDTA (Edetate Disocium)
Chemical Cautery		Silver Nitrate
Cycloplegic	Parasympatholytic	Atropine Sulfate, Homatropine HBr, Cyclopentolate HCL, Scopolamine HBr
Hyperosmotic		Glucose, Soium Chloride, Glycerin
Miotic	Anti-ACHase	
	Parasympathomimetic	Pilocarpine HCL (0.25-0.5% only)
Mucolytic		
Mydriatic	Sympathomimetic Alpha 1 Agonists only	Hydroxyamphetamine HBr, Phenylephrine
Vasoconstrictor	Sympathomimetic Alpha 1 Agonists only	Naphazoline HCL, Tetrahydroxoline HCL, Oxymetazoline HCL

If properly registered with DEA, Therapeutic Optometrists may **possess for administration** no more than 2 vials of prepackaged cocaine 10% eye drops.

OPTOMETRIC GLAUCOMA SPECIALISTS (identified by a license number ending in the letters TG) may prescribe everything a Therapeutic Optometrist may prescribe **and the following drugs:**
1. Appropriate **oral pharmaceutical agents** used for diagnosing and treating visual defects, abnormal conditions, and diseases of the human vision system, including the eye and adnexa, which are included in the following classification or are combinations of agents in the classifications:
   A. One 10-day supply of oral antibiotics;
   B. One 72-hour supply of oral antihistamines;
   C. One 7-day supply of oral nonsteroidal anti-inflammatories;
   D. One 3-day supply of any analgesic in controlled substance Schedules III, IV, and V (if properly registered with DEA); and
2. Antiglaucoma drugs.

Section Four

Texas Pharmacy Act (TPA) and Selected Rules

Section Four

Texas Pharmacy Act (TPA) and Selected Rules

I. **Introduction, Definitions, and Texas State Board of Pharmacy**
   A. The Texas Pharmacy Act is the primary law governing the practice of pharmacy in Texas. The Act establishes the Texas State Board of Pharmacy (TSBP) and provides the Board with certain authorities and responsibilities in regulating the practice of pharmacy. The purpose of the Act and of TSBP is to promote, preserve, and protect the public health, safety, and welfare of Texans.
   B. Definitions (TPA Section 551.003)

> *Study Tip:* When studying laws and rules, it is important to read the definition section usually found at the beginning of a new section.

   Many definitions are consistent in different acts such as "controlled substance," "dangerous drug," "designated agent," "practice of pharmacy," and "practitioner." Over 40 terms are defined in TPA Section 551.003 and some are listed below:
   1. Class A* pharmacy license – community pharmacy.
   2. Class B pharmacy license – nuclear pharmacy.
   3. Class C* pharmacy license – institutional (hospital) pharmacy.
   4. Class D pharmacy license – clinic pharmacy.
   5. Class E* pharmacy license – nonresident pharmacy.
   *Class A, C, and E pharmacies that compound sterile products must be licensed as Class A-S, C-S, and E-S pharmacies. This allows the Board to know which pharmacies are compounding sterile products.
   Note: These classes of pharmacy are found in the law so they are defined here, but TSBP has also created additional classes (Class F, G, and H pharmacies) by TSBP rule. These are specialized pharmacies that are defined and described in Section Seven of this Guide.
   6. Medication order – An order from a practitioner or practitioner's designated agent for administration of a drug or device.

7. Pharmacy – A facility at which a prescription drug or medication order is received, processed, or dispensed.
8. Prescription drug order – An order from a practitioner or practitioner's designated agent to a pharmacist for a drug to be dispensed or an order from a physician assistant or advanced practice registered nurse.

> ***Study Tip:*** *Note that a medication order is for administration of a drug (inpatient setting) and a prescription drug order is for dispensing of a drug (outpatient setting). Orders in a nursing home are considered prescription drug orders as those orders are dispensed by a pharmacy and sent to the nursing home. However, TSBP rules allow for alternative labeling for prescriptions in nursing homes that are similar to medication orders since they are administered. See TSBP Rule 291.33(c)(7)(D) or TFPDL pages G.23-24.*

C. Texas State Board of Pharmacy (TPA Chapter 552)
   1. The Texas State Board of Pharmacy (TSBP) is composed of 11 members:
      a. 7 pharmacists.
      b. 1 pharmacy technician.
      c. 3 public members.
   2. Qualifications.
      a. TSBP must include representation for pharmacists employed in both Class A and Class C pharmacies.
      b. Pharmacist members must be:
         (1) A resident of Texas.
         (2) Licensed for 5 years preceding appointment.
         (3) In good standing with Board.
         (4) Actively practicing pharmacy.
      c. Pharmacist members (and members' spouses) cannot be:
         (1) A lobbyist on behalf of a profession regulated by the Board.
         (2) An officer, employee, or paid consultant to a Texas trade association in the healthcare field.
      d. Public members (and members' spouses) cannot be:
         (1) Registered, certified, or licensed by an occupational regulatory agency (e.g., nurse, physician).

- (2) Employed by or participate in the management of a business or other entity regulated by the Board or receiving funds from the Board.
- (3) An owner or person who controls more than a 10% interest in a business or other entity regulated by the Board or receiving funds from the Board.
- (4) An officer, employee, or paid consultant to a Texas trade association in the healthcare field.
     3. Appointment and Terms of Office.
        a. Appointed by the governor with advice and consent of the Senate.
        b. Appointed for a 6-year term.
        c. May not serve more than 2 consecutive full terms.
  D. Board Powers and Duties; Rulemaking Authority *(See TPA Chapter 554 or TFPDL pages D.10-14 for details.)*
     1. Administering and enforcing the Texas Pharmacy Act and rules and other laws related to the practice of pharmacy.
     2. Regulation of the practice of pharmacy by:
        a. Issuing and renewing licenses.
        b. Determining and issuing standards for recognizing and approving degree requirements of colleges of pharmacy.
        c. Specifying and enforcing the requirements for practical training, including internship.
        d. Regulating the training, qualifications, and employment of pharmacist interns and pharmacy technicians.

Study Tip: Unlike some states, TSBP does not regulate drug wholesalers. They are regulated by the Texas Department of State Health Services. TSBP also does not have the authority to regulate pharmaceutical manufacturers' representatives.

II. Licensing
  A. Licensing of Pharmacists (TPA Chapter 558)
     1. It is unlawful to practice in Texas without a license or to fraudulently obtain a license.

Study Tip: There is no grace period when renewing a pharmacist license. If you fail to renew your license on time, you cannot legally practice.

2. A person may not use the title "Registered Pharmacist" or "R.Ph." or similar words unless the person is licensed to practice pharmacy in the state (Texas).
3. Licensure by Examination.
   a. Qualifications.
      (1) At least 18 years old.
      (2) Completed internship (1500 hours).
      (3) Graduated and received professional practice degree.
      (4) Passed NAPLEX and MPJE (score of 75 is passing).
      (5) Has not had pharmacist license in another state restricted, suspended, revoked, or surrendered. *Note: A person who is enrolled or plans to enroll in school to become a pharmacist (or a pharmacy technician) or prior to taking an examination for licensure who has reason to believe he or she may be ineligible due to a conviction or deferred adjudication for a felony or misdemeanor offense may request a criminal history evaluation letter. See TSBP Rule 281.11 or TFPDL pages D.20-21.*
   b. Examination retake. If an applicant fails the NAPLEX or MPJE, he or she may retake each examination 4 additional times (5 total).
4. Licensure by Reciprocity.
   a. Must provide proof of initial licensure by examination and that current license or any other licenses have not been suspended, revoked, cancelled, surrendered, or otherwise restricted.
   b. Must pass the Texas MPJE (score of 75 is passing).
   c. Texas allows a pharmacist to reciprocate his or her license from a state where a pharmacist obtained a license by examination or reciprocity.
5. Special rules apply for licenses for military service members, military veterans, and military spouses. *See TSBP Rule 283.12.*
6. Internship.
   a. Pharmacist intern – An intern trainee, a student intern, a resident intern, or an extended intern who is participating in a Board-approved internship program.

b. Intern trainee – An individual registered with the Board who is enrolled in the first professional year in a Texas college/school of pharmacy and who may work in a site assigned by the school.
c. Student intern – An individual registered with the Board who has successfully completed the first professional year (minimum of 30 credit hours). Student intern designation expires if the person:
   (1) Ceases enrollment at accredited school/college.
   (2) Fails NAPLEX and/or Texas MPJE.
   (3) Fails to take NAPLEX and/or Texas MPJE within 6 calendar months after graduation.
d. Resident intern – An individual registered with the Board who has graduated from a college/school of pharmacy and is completing an accredited residency program.
e. Extended intern – An individual registered with the Board who is no longer a student intern and other individuals in specific circumstances such as foreign pharmacy graduates or those seeking reissuance of a pharmacist license.
f. Goal and objectives of internship – The goal of internship is for the pharmacist intern to attain the knowledge, skills, and abilities to safely, efficiently, and effectively provide pharmacist-delivered patient care to a diverse patient population and practice pharmacy under the laws and regulations of the state of Texas. Some of the objectives are as follows:
   (1) Providing drug products.
   (2) Communicating with patients about prescription drugs.
   (3) Communicating with patients about nonprescription drugs, devices, dietary supplements, diet, nutrition, traditional nondrug therapy, complementary and alternative therapies, and diagnostic aids.
   (4) Communicating with healthcare professionals.
   (5) Practicing as part of the patient's interdisciplinary healthcare team.
   (6) Maintaining professional ethical standards.

(7) Compounding.
(8) Retrieving and evaluating drug information.
(9) Managing general pharmacy operations.
(10) Participating in public health, community service, or professional activities.
(11) Demonstrating scientific inquiry.

Note: The details of the objectives of internship can be found in TSBP Rule 283.4 or TFPDL pages D.27-29.

g. Intern Duties (TSBP Rule 283.5 or TFPDL page D.32).
  (1) Pharmacist interns (includes intern trainees, student interns, extended interns, and likely resident interns, although the TSBP rule has not been updated to include resident interns) may perform any duty of a pharmacist provided they are working under the supervision of a pharmacist registered as a preceptor or a healthcare professional preceptor.

  Note: A healthcare professional preceptor may be a physician, dentist, podiatrist, veterinarian, advanced practice registered nurse, or physician assistant in Texas or another state; or a pharmacist in a state other than Texas but not licensed in Texas who is serving as an instructor for a Texas college/school-based internship program and who is recognized by a Texas college/school of pharmacy to supervise and be responsible for the activities and functions of a pharmacist intern.

  (2) While intern trainees may perform any duty of a pharmacist just as other interns, they can only do so at locations where they have been assigned by a Texas college or school of pharmacy.
  (3) Interns may not present themselves as a pharmacist, sign documents that require a pharmacist to sign (such as controlled substance invoices), or supervise technicians.
  (4) When not working under the supervision of a preceptor, an intern functions as a pharmacy technician (must have completed the pharmacy's technician training program) but does not count in any ratio of pharmacy technicians to pharmacists.

> *Study Tip:* Be familiar with the duties an intern can perform that a technician cannot, such as patient counseling and receiving new prescriptions.

      h. Hour Requirements.
         (1) 1500 hours required by TSBP rule.
         (2) An intern cannot receive credit for more than 50 hours per week.
      i. Preceptors (TSBP Rule 283.6. or TFPDL pages D.32-33).
         (1) Must have a current, active pharmacist license.
         (2) Must have at least 1 year of experience or 6 months of residency training.
         (3) Must have completed 3 hours of preceptor training through an ACPE course.
         (4) Must complete 3 hours of preceptor training every 2 years.
         (5) Must have a license that has not been disciplined.
         (6) In addition to pharmacist preceptors, preceptors may also be healthcare professionals (physicians, dentists, veterinarians, or pharmacists licensed in other states serving as an instructor for a Texas college/school of pharmacy).
         (7) A preceptor may only supervise one intern. However, the 1:1 ratio does not apply to intern trainees or student interns that are part of a Texas college/school of pharmacy program. In such a program, supervision must be direct for dispensing activities and general supervision for other activities.

> *Study Tip:* There is no ratio for preceptors supervising pharmacist interns as a part of a Texas college/school of pharmacy program.

  B. License Renewal (TPA Chapter 559)
    1. Licenses shall be renewed annually or biennially (TSBP now renews biennially).
    2. Licenses expire on the last day of the assigned month (birth month).

3. "Timely receipt" of renewal application and fee means received in the Board's office on the last day of the expiration month. There is no grace period. Most people now renew online.
4. If a license is expired for fewer than 90 days, the licensee may renew the license by paying a renewal fee that is equal to one and one-half times the renewal fee and report required hours of continuing education (CE).
5. If a license is expired for more than 90 days but less than one year, the licensee may pay a renewal fee equal to two times the renewal fee and report the required number of CE hours. *Remember: You cannot practice if your license is expired.*
6. After one year, the license cannot be renewed, but see TSBP Rule 283.10 or TFPDL page D.39 for alternatives to re-examination.
7. Inactive Status (TSBP Rule 295.9 or TFPDL pages D.47-48). Pharmacists who cannot renew their license because they do not have the required continuing education requirements can place their license in inactive status.

Study Tip: You cannot practice while your license is inactive, and you must still pay the license renewal fee. To activate your license, you must pay a fee and meet specific CE requirements.

C. Continuing Education (CE)
1. To renew a pharmacist license, a pharmacist must complete at least 30 contact hours of CE (3.0 CEUs) during the preceding license period (2 years) with at least 1 contact hour (0.1 CEU) related to Texas pharmacy laws and rules and 1 contact hour (0.1 CEU) related to opioid abuse.
2. Methods of Obtaining CE.
   a. Any Accreditation Council for Pharmacy Education (ACPE) accredited course.

Study Tip: ACPE uses Continuing Education Units (CEUs) to accredit courses, but TSBP (and nearly every organization) refers to Continuing Education contact hours. Be sure you know that one contact hour equals 0.1 CEU (1 hour = 0.1 CEU).

b. Successfully completing, during the preceding license period, one credit hour for each year of his or her license period, which is part of the professional degree program (accredited by ACPE) in a college of pharmacy. (This would include people in a nontraditional Pharm.D. program.)
c. Taking and passing the standardized pharmacy examination (NAPLEX) during the preceding license period, which shall be equivalent to 30 contact hours of continuing education.
d. In addition to ACPE accredited courses, TSBP allows other methods for obtaining CE that can be found under Approved Programs in TSBP Rule 295.8 or TFPDL pages D.43-46. These include:
    (1) Completing courses that are part of the professional degree program of a college of pharmacy.
    (2) Completing a cardiopulmonary resuscitation (CPR) course (1 hour).
    (3) Completing Advanced Cardiac Life Support courses leading to initial certification (12 hours).
    (4) Completing Advanced Cardiac Life Support courses leading to recertification (4 hours).
    (5) Attending a Texas State Board of Pharmacy meeting (3 hours).
    (6) Participating in a Texas State Board of Pharmacy appointed Task Force (3 hours).
    (7) Attending programs presented by the Texas State Board of Pharmacy.
    (8) Completing an Institute for Safe Medication Practices Medication Safety Self-Assessment (3 hours).
    (9) Passing a certain Board of Pharmaceutical Specialties certification examination administered by the Board of Pharmaceutical Specialties (3 hours).
    (10) Completing programs accredited by Accreditation Council for Continuing Medical Education as Category 1 Continuing Medical Education (CME).
e. Must keep CE records for 3 years.

> ***Study Tip:*** *CE records are the only records that TSBP requires to be kept for 3 years. Most other records are required to be kept for 2 years.*

    3. CPE Monitoring Service.
        a. The CPE Monitoring Service is a joint effort of ACPE and NABP which allows pharmacists to electronically track pharmacist continuing education from ACPE accredited providers.
        b. Pharmacists should set up an NABP e-profile at NABP's CPE Monitor website and obtain an e-profile ID. The CPE Monitor e-profile ID should be provided when obtaining continuing education from an ACPE accredited provider.

D. Licensing of Pharmacies (TPA Chapter 560)
    1. The use of the term "Pharmacy" or "Apothecary" in a business that would lead the public to believe that the business is a pharmacy is not permitted unless the business is a licensed pharmacy.
    2. A separate license is required for each location.
    3. Only one license may be issued to a location. If a hospital is operating a Class A pharmacy under its Class C license, it is not required to have a Class A license. However, it must follow Class A rules for the outpatient pharmacy including the Class A ratio of pharmacy technicians to pharmacists.
    4. There are detailed requirements for a pharmacy license application that can be found in TSBP Rule 291.1 or TFPDL pages D.51-52. Some of the requirements include the signature of the pharmacist-in-charge, notarized signature of the owner, an approved credit application from a primary drug wholesaler, and business formation documents. An on-site inspection is also required prior to issuing a license. However, TSBP can waive that requirement if the applicant holds another active pharmacy license in the state or for another good reason.
    5. Any pharmacy that compounds sterile products cannot be licensed by TSBP until the pharmacy has been inspected by TSBP.
    6. A pharmacy that fails to engage in the business as described in the application for a license within 6 months of the date of issuance of the license is subject to disciplinary action. *See TSBP Rule 291.11 or TFPDL page F.15.*

7. A pharmacy license is not transferable. If there is a change of location or change of name, the pharmacy must file a new application and return the old license. TSBP actually issues an amended license (the previous license number does not change). For a change of location, TSBP must be notified in writing at least 30 days before the change.
8. TSBP is prohibited by law from adopting rules regarding ratios of pharmacy technicians to pharmacists in Class C pharmacies. *hospital*

III. **Generic Drug Substitution and Interchangeable Biological Products (Texas Pharmacy Act Chapter 562 Subchapter A and Board of Pharmacy Rule 309)**
   A. Definitions
      1. Generically Equivalent – A drug that is pharmaceutically equivalent and therapeutically equivalent.
      2. Pharmaceutically Equivalent – Drug products having identical amounts of the same active chemical ingredient in the same dosage form.
      3. Therapeutically Equivalent – Pharmaceutically equivalent drugs that when administered in the same amounts will provide the same therapeutic effect, identical in duration and intensity.
      4. Interchangeable – Means a biological product that is designated as biosimilar and therapeutically equivalent to another product approved by the FDA.
     Note: The Texas statute refers to biological product designation as equivalent in the FDA Orange Book, but the publication FDA uses for therapeutic equivalency evaluations for biologicals is the FDA Purple Book.
   B. Permissive Substitution – A pharmacist may dispense a generically equivalent drug or interchangeable biological product if:
      1. The product costs less than the brand name prescribed.
      2. The patient does not refuse the substitution.
      3. The prescriber has not prohibited substitution by a dispensing directive.
   C. Dispensing Directive
      1. Written Prescriptions.
         a. A practitioner may prohibit the substitution of a

generically equivalent drug or interchangeable biological product by writing across the face of the prescription, in the practitioner's own handwriting, the phrase "brand necessary" or "brand medically necessary."
    b. Two-line prescription forms, check boxes, or other notations on an original prescription drug order which indicate "substitution instructions" are not valid methods to prohibit substitution, and a pharmacist may substitute on these types of prescriptions.
    c. The dispensing directive may not be preprinted, rubber-stamped, or otherwise reproduced on the prescription.

2. Verbal Prescriptions.
    a. A practitioner may prohibit the substitution of a generically equivalent drug or interchangeable biological product by specifying "brand necessary" or "brand medically necessary."
    b. On a verbal prescription for a Medicaid patient, the practitioner must also mail or fax a written prescription with the written dispensing directive to the pharmacy within 30 days.

3. Electronic Prescriptions.
    a. A practitioner may prohibit the substitution of a generically equivalent drug or interchangeable biological product by noting "brand necessary" or "brand medically necessary" on the electronic prescription.
    b. On an electronic prescription for a Medicaid patient, the practitioner must also mail or fax a written prescription with the written dispensing directive to the pharmacy within 30 days.

4. Out-of-State Prescriptions. For out-of-state, Canadian, or Mexican practitioners or practitioners in federal facilities, the prescription must authorize substitution (rather than prohibit it).

D. Pharmacist's Responsibilities
1. Patient Notification. Must inform patient that a less expensive generically equivalent drug or interchangeable biological is available for the brand prescribed. In addition, the pharmacist or his or her agent must ask the patient or the patient's agent to choose between the generically

equivalent drug/interchangeable biological product and the brand prescribed.
2. Communication with Prescriber. Not later than 3 days after dispensing a biological product, the dispensing pharmacist or designee shall communicate to the prescribing practitioner the specific product provided to the patient, including the name of the product and the manufacturer or NDC number. This can be done making an entry into a medical records system or prescription claim system that is accessible to the prescriber.
Note: The physician notification is only required if the biological product dispensed has been substituted for the prescribed product. This requirement expires on September 1, 2019.
3. Selection of Drug Products. The determination of the drug or biological product to be dispensed is the professional responsibility of the pharmacist. For drugs listed in *Approved Drug Products With Therapeutic Equivalents* (the FDA Orange Book), the pharmacist may only substitute "A" rated drugs. For drugs not listed in the FDA Orange Book, the pharmacist may use professional discretion. Biological products must be listed as interchangeable in the FDA Purple Book.
4. Labeling. The prescription label must include "Substituted for Brand Prescribed" or "Substituted for 'Brand Name'" where 'Brand Name' is the name of the actual product prescribed.

E. Substitution of Dosage Form
1. A pharmacist may dispense, with the patient's consent and notification to the prescriber, a dosage form of a drug product different from that prescribed, such as a tablet instead of a capsule or a liquid instead of tablets.
2. Requirements.
   a. Must contain the identical amount of the active ingredient as the dosage prescribed.
   b. Is not an enteric-coated or timed-release product.
   c. Does not alter clinical outcomes.

IV. Other Provisions of Texas Pharmacy Act
A. Display of Pharmacy License (TPA Section 562.103)
1. Pharmacies shall display their pharmacy license in public view.
Note: *Pharmacists and technicians are no longer required to post their licenses or renewal certificates.*

2. Class A and C pharmacies must display the word "pharmacy" or similar word or symbol in front of the pharmacy if they serve the general public.
3. A pharmacy shall make available to the public on request proof that each pharmacist, pharmacist intern, pharmacy technician, and pharmacy technician trainee holds the appropriate license or registration.

> ***Study Tip:*** *You cannot copy your original license or renewal certificate, but you may copy your "pocket license" card.*

B. Emergency Refills (TPA Section 562.054 and TSBP Rule 291.34(b)(8) (D) and (E)) – A pharmacist may exercise professional judgment in refilling a prescription for a drug, other than a Schedule II controlled substance, without authorization of the prescriber if:
  1. Failure to refill the prescription might result in an interruption of a therapeutic regimen or create patient suffering.
  2. Either a natural or manmade disaster has occurred that prohibits the pharmacist from being able to contact the prescriber or the pharmacist is unable to contact the prescriber after reasonable effort.
  3. The quantity of the prescription drug dispensed does not exceed a 72-hour supply.
  4. If the Governor declares a disaster and if notified by TSBP, the pharmacist may dispense a 30-day supply.
  5. By policy, TSBP permits dispensing the entire unit-of-use products such as oral contraceptives, inhalers, and ophthalmic solutions.
  6. The pharmacist informs the patient at the time of dispensing that the refill is being provided without the prescriber's authorization and that the authorization of the prescriber is required for future refills, and
     a. The pharmacist informs the practitioner of the emergency refill at the earliest reasonable time.
     b. The pharmacist maintains a record of the emergency refill containing the information required to be maintained on a prescription.
     c. The pharmacist labels the refill as a prescription.

Study Tip: Remember that the emergency refill rules apply to Schedule III-V drugs also. Since DEA has not issued an opinion on this under federal law, pharmacists should exercise professional judgment applying the emergency refill rules to Schedule III-V controlled substances. For purposes of exam preparation, since Texas rules specifically allow this, the rules can be applied to emergency refills for Schedule III-V products.

C. Auto-Refill Programs
   1. Pharmacies may use a program that automatically refills prescriptions that have existing refills available to improve patient compliance with and adherence to prescribed medication therapy.
   2. Patients must affirmatively indicate that they wish to enroll in such a program, and the pharmacy shall document such indication.
   3. Patients must have the option to withdraw from such a program at any time.
   4. Auto-refill programs may be used for refills of dangerous drugs and Schedule IV and V controlled substances. Schedule II and III controlled substances may not be dispensed by an auto-refill program.

Study Tip: It makes sense that auto-refills for Schedule II prescriptions are not allowed for Schedule II prescriptions since refills of Schedule II controlled substances are not allowed, but this rule also prohibits auto-refills of Schedule III prescriptions.

D. 90-Day Supply and Accelerated Refills – A pharmacist may dispense up to a 90-day supply of a dangerous drug (no controlled substances) from a prescription that specifies for a lesser amount if:
   1. The total quantity dispensed doesn't exceed the total prescribed (including refills).
   2. The patient consents to the dispensing.
   3. The physician has been notified electronically or by telephone.
   4. The drug is not a psychotropic drug.
   5. The patient is at least 18 years of age.

Study Tip: Prior to this law, a pharmacist could not advance refills on a prescription without calling the prescriber to change the quantity. If all the conditions are met, a pharmacist can now do this and then notify the prescriber afterward.

E. Bioterrorism, Epidemic, or Pandemic Disease Reporting
   1. A pharmacist shall report to the Texas Department of State Health Services any unusual or increased prescription rates or trends that may be caused by bioterrorism, epidemic, or pandemic disease.
   2. These include an increase in the number of prescriptions (including antibiotics) to treat respiratory or gastrointestinal complaints and sales of over-the-counter products to treat respiratory or gastrointestinal complaints or fever.

F. Administration of Epinephrine
   1. A pharmacist may administer epinephrine through an auto-injector in an emergency.
   2. The law also provides liability protection for a pharmacist who in good faith administers epinephrine in accordance with this section.
   3. Immediately after administering the epinephrine, the pharmacist shall ensure that 911 is called and the patient is evaluated by emergency medical personnel.
   4. A pharmacist must report such administration to the patient's primary care physician within 72 hours from the time of administration.

G. Required Notifications to TSBP

Required Report	Who Reports	Time Frame	Source
Change of pharmacist name or address	Pharmacist	Within 10 days	Rule 295.1
Change of pharmacist employment	Pharmacist	Within 10 days	Rule 291.3(e)
Permanent closing of pharmacy	Pharmacy	Within 10 days after closing	TPA 562.106 and Rule 291.5
Change of pharmacy ownership	Pharmacy	Within 10 days and new license required	TPA 562.106 and Rule 291.3(d)
Change of pharmacy location	Pharmacy	New license filed 30 days prior to change	TPA 562.106 and Rule 291.3(a)
Change of pharmacy name	Pharmacy	New license filed 10 days prior to change	Rule 291.3(b)
Change of managing officers or partnership/corporation	Pharmacy	Within 10 days	Rule 291.3(c)
Change of pharmacist-in-charge (PIC)	Incoming PIC	Within 10 days	TPA 562.106 and Rule 291.3(e)(2)
Sale or transfer of drugs as a result of closing or change of ownership	Pharmacy	Within 10 days	TPA 562.106
Fire or other disaster, accident, or emergency that may affect the strength, purity, or labeling of a drug, medical device	Pharmacy/PIC	Within 10 days	TPA 562.106 and Rule 291.3(g)
Significant loss or theft of controlled substances or dangerous drugs	Pharmacy	Immediately upon discovery	Rule 291.3(f)
Significant loss of data from pharmacy computer system	Pharmacy	Within 10 days	Records requirements are in each Class of Pharmacy rules
A licensee or registrant obtaining dangerous drugs or controlled substances from a forged prescription	Pharmacy	Immediately upon discovery	Rule 291.3(i)
A final order against the pharmacy license holder or pharmacist-in-charge by the regulatory or licensing agency of the state in which the pharmacy is located if in another state.	Pharmacy	Within 10 days	TPA 561.106 and Rule 291.3(j)

H. Administration and Provision of Dangerous Drugs by Physicians (TPA Chapter 563 or TFPDL pages D.83-84)
  1. Texas generally does not permit physician dispensing.
  2. Exceptions.
     a. A physician may provide a 72-hour supply of dangerous drugs (no controlled substances) to a patient in the physician's office to meet the patient's immediate therapeutic needs.
     b. Physicians in certain rural areas and where there is no pharmacy may dispense dangerous drugs to patients and be reimbursed for the cost.
     c. Veterinarians are allowed to dispense to their own patients without being licensed as a pharmacy.
I. Impaired Pharmacists/Pharmacy Students Program and Peer Review Program (TPA Chapter 564 or TFPDL pages D.84-86)
  1. Impaired Pharmacists/Pharmacy Students Program.
     a. Pharmacists and pharmacy students who have an alcohol or drug impairment can enter into treatment and monitoring through the Professional Recovery Network (PRN).
     b. Individuals who enter the program voluntarily are not reported to TSBP as long as they follow through with PRN's recommendations.
     c. Pharmacists and technicians may also be placed into the PRN program as part of the disciplinary process by TSBP.
     d. Any board order by TSBP related to impairment is confidential.
     e. The program is partially funded by a surcharge on all pharmacy and pharmacist licenses. However, the funds only pay for evaluation of participants. They do not cover the cost for treatment.
  2. Peer Review Program.
     a. A Peer Review committee may be set up by pharmacy owners or pharmacy associations to evaluate the quality of care in pharmacies by reviewing errors or near errors or other quality issues.
     b. In an effort to encourage pharmacies to establish these committees, the statute provides legal protection in civil litigation to peer review documents.
     c. Setting up a peer review committee is voluntary.

However, some pharmacies may be mandated to establish a committee as part of the disciplinary action against the pharmacy license (usually as a result of a medication error).
J. Reporting Professional Liability Claims (TSBP Rule 281.18 or TFPDL pages D.100-103)
   1. An insurer who provides professional liability insurance to pharmacists, pharmacy technicians, or pharmacies must report to TSBP any claim filed against a pharmacist, pharmacy technician, or pharmacy related to care that results in injury or death.
   2. If a pharmacist, pharmacy technician, or pharmacy does not have professional liability insurance and receives such a legal claim, the individual must report the claim to TSBP.
   3. The initial report is required within 30 days of receiving the claim notice. A follow-up report is required within 105 days after disposition (settlement, dismissal, judgment, etc.) of the claim.

V. **Pharmacy Technicians and Pharmacy Technician Trainees (TPA Chapter 568)**
   A. Registration Required (TSBP Rule 297.3 or TFPDL pages D.87-91)
      1. Must be registered as a technician or technician trainee prior to beginning work in a pharmacy.
      2. Technician trainee registration is valid for 2 years and is not renewable.
      3. Initial registration as a technician requires passing a Board approved certification examination, but maintaining certification is not required for renewal of registration.
      4. Renewal of registration requires 20 hours of continuing education (every 2 years) including 1 hour of Texas law. *See TSBP Rule 297.8 or TFPDL pages D.94-98.*
   B. Ratios
      1. Ratio of pharmacists to pharmacy technicians in a Class A pharmacy is 1:4 as long as at least one of the technicians is a registered technician (cannot have 4 trainees). If all are trainees, the ratio is 1:3.
      2. There is no ratio in Class C Pharmacies.
   C. Training
      1. Pharmacy technicians and technician trainees must complete training conducted by the pharmacist-in-charge as outlined in a technician training manual.

        2. Specific requirements for the training manual can be found in TSBP Rule 297.6 or TFPDL pages D.92-93.
        3. The pharmacist-in-charge must document such training.
    D. Continuing Education (CE)
        1. Pharmacy technicians (but not trainees) are required to complete 20 contact hours of continuing education every 2 years to renew their registration.
        2. At least one hour must be related to Texas pharmacy laws and rules.
        3. Acceptable forms of CE are the same as those for pharmacists and also include pharmacy related courses as part of a pharmacy technician training program.
        4. Pharmacy technicians who maintain their certification are considered to have met CE requirements and are not subject to audit by TSBP.

VI. Miscellaneous Texas Pharmacy Act Provisions and TSBP Rules
    A. Immunizations and Vaccinations (TSBP Rule 295.15 or TFPDL pages D.16-19)
        1. Requires written protocol with a physician.
        2. Services to patients under age 14 may be provided only if referred by a physician except that a pharmacist may administer an influenza vaccination to a patient over the age of 7 without an established physician-patient relationship.
        3. May only be given at a pharmacy or location provided in the protocol; cannot be provided where patient resides except for nursing homes or hospitals.
        4. Pharmacist certification requires an ACPE approved course which includes:
            a. Basic Cardiac Life Support Certification.
            b. 20 hours of CDC training.
            c. 3 hours of CE every 2 years relating to disease states, drugs, and administration of immunizations or vaccines.
        5. Notifications.
            a. Pharmacist must notify physician who issued the protocol within 24 hours of administration and
            b. The primary care physician of the patient must be notified within 14 days of administration.
    B. Drug Therapy Management (DTM) Under Protocol (TSBP Rule 295.13 or TFPDL pages E.2-5)

1. Pharmacists may perform drug therapy management as authorized by a physician under a written protocol.
2. Drug therapy management may include:
   a. Collecting and reviewing patient drug use histories.
   b. Ordering or performing routine drug therapy related patient assessment procedures such as temperature, pulse, and respiration.
   c. Ordering drug therapy related laboratory tests.
   d. Implementing or modifying drug therapy following diagnosis, initial patient assessment, and ordering of drug therapy by a physician as detailed in the protocol.
   e. Signing a prescription drug order for a dangerous drug (no controlled substances) if:
      (1) The delegation follows a diagnosis, initial patient assessment, and drug therapy order by the physician,
      (2) The pharmacist practices in a hospital, hospital-based clinic, or an academic healthcare institution, and
      (3) The hospital, hospital-based clinic, or academic healthcare institution in which the pharmacist practices has bylaws and a medical staff policy that permit a physician to delegate to a pharmacist the management of a patient's drug therapy.

Study Tip: Drug therapy management can take place at any location, but the signing of a prescription drug order by a pharmacist under drug therapy management is restricted to specific sites, as indicated in e. above.

   f. Any other drug therapy related act delegated by a physician.
3. Written Protocol.
   a. Must identify the supervising physician and the pharmacist authorized to perform DTM.
   b. Must identify types of DTM decisions the pharmacist is authorized to make.
   c. Must state activities the pharmacist shall follow in performing DTM.
   d. Must state mechanisms and time schedule for pharmacist to report to physician.

4. Notification and CE Requirements.
    a. Must notify TSBP prior to engaging in DTM.
    b. Must complete at least 6 hours of CE annually related to drug therapy.
5. Supervision.
    a. Physician must review protocol and any deviations from protocol at least annually.
    b. Physician must have physician-patient relationship with each patient.
    c. Physician must be geographically located to be physically present daily.
    d. Physician must receive periodic status reports on a schedule defined in the protocol.
    e. Physician must be available through telecommunication for consultation.

Study Tip: There is no limit to the number of physicians for whom a pharmacist may perform drug therapy management, and there is no limit to the number of pharmacists with whom a physician can enter into a protocol.

6. Records.
    a. Must be kept for 2 years.
    b. Must keep a copy of the written protocol and any patient specific deviations from the protocol.
    c. Must document all interventions.
    d. Must review protocol annually.
C. Inventory Requirements (TSBP Rule 291.17 or TFPDL pages E.15-18)
    1. General Requirements.
        a. PIC is responsible for ensuring all inventories are taken.
        b. Inventories must be maintained in pharmacy, filed separately from other records, and be available for inspection for 2 years.
        c. Inventories include all stock "on hand" of controlled substances (including expired drugs).
        d. Persons taking inventory and PIC shall sign and date the inventory and indicate the time inventory was taken.
        e. The signature of the PIC and date of the inventory shall be notarized within 72 hours or 3 working days for all

inventories except for the initial inventory and change in PIC inventory.
- f. The PIC is responsible for making an exact count of all Schedule II controlled substances.
- g. The PIC is also responsible for making an estimated count of Schedule III-V controlled substances provided the container has fewer than 1000 tablets or capsules.
- h. Schedule II controlled substances shall be listed separately.
- i. If a pharmacy maintains a perpetual inventory, it must be reconciled on the date of the annual inventory.

2. Required Inventories.
   - a. Initial inventory – If on the opening day of business there are no controlled substances, then record zero.
   - b. Annual inventory – An annual inventory of controlled substances is required in Texas in contrast to the DEA every two year inventory requirement.
   - c. Change of Ownership of Class A, A-S, C, C-S, or F Pharmacy.
     - (1) Inventory shall be taken on the date of change of ownership.
     - (2) Constitutes closing inventory for seller and the initial inventory for buyer.
   - d. Change of PIC of Class A, A-S, C, C-S or F Pharmacy.

3. Perpetual Inventories.
   - a. Class C and C-S pharmacies must maintain a perpetual inventory for Schedule II controlled substances.
   - b. Class C Ambulatory Care Facility pharmacies and Class F (Freestanding Emergency Medical Center) pharmacies must maintain a perpetual inventory for all controlled substances.
   - c. All pharmacies must maintain a perpetual inventory of any controlled substances stored at a remote location.

Study Tip: *Although many Class A and A-S pharmacies maintain a perpetual inventory of all controlled substances, it is important to know that they are not required (other than for those stored in remote pharmacy locations). Similarly, many Class C and C-S pharmacies keep a perpetual inventory of all controlled substances but are only required to do so for Schedule II drugs.*

D. Closing a Pharmacy (TSBP Rule 291.5 or TFPDL pages E.10-12)

> *Study Tip:* This rules applies when closing a pharmacy and no further pharmacy activities will take place at the location. If a pharmacy is being sold and pharmacy activities will continue at the location, the rules for change of ownership should be followed. Those rules include applying for a new pharmacy license as well as DEA notification, inventory, and transfer requirements.

1. Prior to Closing. At least 14 days prior to closing, the PIC must:
   a. Notify DEA.
   b. Post a closing notice informing patients of the name, address, and telephone number of the pharmacy acquiring the records.
2. Closing Day. The PIC must:
   a. Take a closing inventory.
   b. Transfer prescription drug order files and patient medication records.
   c. Remove all signs that indicate the location is a pharmacy.
3. After Closing.
   a. Within 10 days after closing, the PIC must provide to TSBP a written notice of the actual date of closing, the pharmacy license, a statement that an inventory was conducted per TSBP Rule 291.17, the manner in which dangerous drugs and controlled substances were transferred or disposed, and the name and address of the pharmacy to which records were transferred.
   b. If the pharmacy is registered to possess controlled substances, a notification must be sent to a DEA divisional office explaining that the pharmacy has closed along with the DEA registration certificate and any unused DEA Forms 222 which have been voided.

E. Remote Pharmacy Services (TSBP Rule 291.121 or TFPDL pages D.76-81)

TPA and TSBP rules recognize three types of remote pharmacy practices in which drugs may be stored and/or dispensed from locations where a pharmacist is not present. These three types of remote pharmacy practices include Emergency Medication Kits at nursing homes, Automated Pharmacy Systems for routine dispensing of drugs at certain healthcare facilities including nursing homes, and Telepharmacy Systems used for dispensing drugs at remote dispensing sites and certain remote healthcare sites.

Note: At the time of publication of this guide, TSBP adopted Rule 291.121(d) creating a fourth type of remote pharmacy practice for pharmacy automated storage and delivery systems (kiosks) at locations outside of a pharmacy. (See Study Tip on page 151.) The Remote Pharmacy Practice rules are not the rules for remote order entry. The rules for remote order entry can be found in the Centralized Prescription Drug and Medication Order Processing TSBP Rule 291.153.

1. Summary of TSBP Rule 291.121(b) Remote Pharmacy Services Using an Emergency Medication Kit.
    a. This rule allows a Class A or C pharmacy or a Class E pharmacy located within 20 miles of a facility to provide pharmacy services to facilities licensed under Health and Safety Code Chapter 242 (Convalescent Homes, Nursing Homes, and Related Institutions) or Chapter 252 (Intermediate Care Facilities for the Mentally Retarded) using an Emergency Medication Kit as outlined in Section 562.108 of the Texas Pharmacy Act. It also allows a U.S. Department of Veterans Affairs pharmacy or other federally operated pharmacy to provide pharmacy services using an Emergency Medical Kit at an institution licensed under Chapter 242 that is a Texas State Veterans Home.
    b. An application to TSBP is required before providing these services.
    c. DEA Rule 1301.27(b) requires automated dispensing systems in long term care facilities to be registered with DEA. However, if the automated system is being used solely as an emergency kit and not for routine dispensing of controlled substances, a DEA registration is not required.
    d. Access to the emergency medication kit is limited to pharmacists and healthcare personnel employed by the facility.
    e. Contents of the emergency medication kit shall be determined by the consultant pharmacist, pharmacist-in-charge of the provider pharmacy, medical director, and

director of nursing and shall be limited to those drugs necessary to meet the resident's emergency medication needs. This refers to a situation in which a drug cannot be supplied by a pharmacy within a reasonable time.

> ***Study Tip:*** *Texas does not have specific quantity limits or a list of specific drugs that can be stored in an emergency medication kit.*

      f. Stocking of drugs in an automated pharmacy system must be done by a pharmacist, pharmacy technician, or pharmacy technician trainee unless the system uses barcoding, microchip, or other technologies to ensure that the containers or unit-dose drugs are accurately loaded and other specific requirements are met.

      g. A record must be maintained of all drugs sent to and returned from the remote location and should be kept separate from the records of the provider pharmacy and from other remote site records.

      h. A perpetual inventory of all controlled substances must be maintained for each remote location, and each remote location's controlled substances must be inventoried on the same day as the provider pharmacy's inventory.

2. Summary of TSBP Rule 291.121(a) Remote Pharmacy Services Using Automated Pharmacy Systems (primarily in nursing homes).

    a. This rule allows a Class A or C pharmacy to provide pharmacy services to facilities licensed under Health and Safety Code Chapter 142 (Home and Community Support Service Agencies including hospices), Chapter 242 (Convalescent Homes, Nursing Homes, and Related Institutions), Chapter 247 (Assisted Living Facilities), and Chapter 252 (Intermediate Care Facilities for the Mentally Retarded) as well as jails or prisons operated by the State of Texas or local government.

    b. Drugs may only be maintained in an automated pharmacy system.

    c. If controlled substances are to be stored and dispensed from the automated system at the remote location, a DEA registration must be obtained for the remote location in the name of the pharmacy providing the remote pharmacy services.

d. An application to TSBP is required prior to providing these services.
e. A pharmacist may supervise operation of the system electronically, and a pharmacist shall control all operations of the automated pharmacy system and approve the release of the initial dose after receiving a valid prescription drug order.
f. Drugs dispensed using the automated pharmacy system must meet the labeling requirements or alternative labeling requirements found in TSBP Rule 291.33(c).
g. Drugs used in the automated pharmacy system must be in the original manufacturer's container or be prepackaged in the provider pharmacy.
h. Stocking of drugs in an automated pharmacy system must be done by a pharmacist, pharmacy technician, or pharmacy technician trainee unless the system uses removable cartridges or containers and other specific requirements are met.
i. A record must be maintained of all drugs sent to and returned from the remote location and should be kept separate from the records of the provider pharmacy and from other remote site records.
j. A perpetual inventory of all controlled substances must be maintained for each remote location, and each remote location's controlled substances must be inventoried on the same day as the provider pharmacy's inventory.

3. Summary of TSBP Rule 291.121(c) Remote Pharmacy Services Using Telepharmacy Systems.
    a. These provisions allow a Class A or C pharmacy to provide pharmacy services to a rural health clinic regulated under 42 U.S.C. Section 1395x(aa), a health center as defined by 42 U.S.C. Section 254b (serving medically underserved populations), or a healthcare facility located in a medically underserved area as defined by state or federal law. It also allows a Class A pharmacy (but not a Class C pharmacy) to provide telepharmacy services at remote dispensing sites staffed by a pharmacy technician.

b. A telepharmacy system is a system that monitors the dispensing of prescription drugs and provides for related drug use regimen and patient counseling services by an electronic method which includes the use of audio and video, still image capture, and store and forward.
c. Legislation passed in 2017 that expanded the use of telepharmacy beyond healthcare clinics and facilities includes "remote dispensing sites."
   (1) A remote dispensing site is defined as a location licensed as a telepharmacy that is authorized by a provider pharmacy through a telepharmacy system to store and dispense drugs and devices including dangerous drugs and controlled substances.
   (2) A remote dispensing site must be staffed by an onsite pharmacy technician who is under the continuous supervision of a pharmacist employed by the provider pharmacy.
   (3) Pharmacy technicians at a remote dispensing site must have worked at least 1 year at a retail pharmacy during the past 3 years and must complete a Board-approved training program on the proper use of a telepharmacy system.
   (4) Pharmacy technicians at a remote dispensing site are included in the pharmacist-pharmacy technician ratio of the provider pharmacy and may not perform extemporaneous sterile or nonsterile compounding, but may prepare commercially available medications for dispensing including reconstitution of orally administered powder antibiotics.
   (5) Only a Class A pharmacy may serve as a provider pharmacy for a remote dispensing site.
   (6) A provider pharmacy may provide pharmacy services at no more than 2 remote dispensing sites.
   (7) A remote dispensing site may not be located within 22 road miles of a Class A pharmacy. If a Class A pharmacy opens within that mileage restriction after a remote dispensing site is operating, the remote dispensing site may continue to operate.

(8) A remote dispensing site may not dispense Schedule II controlled substances.
(9) If a remote dispensing site dispenses an average of more than 125 prescriptions each day the site is open (calculated annually), it must apply for a Class A license.
(10) A pharmacist employed by a provider pharmacy must make at least monthly onsite visits to a remote dispensing site and must reconcile the perpetual inventory of controlled substances to the on-hand count at the remote dispensing site.
d. If controlled substances are to be stored at the remote location, a DEA registration must be obtained for the remote location.
e. Drugs dispensed at a remote site through a telepharmacy system may only be delivered to the patient at the remote site.
f. A pharmacy may not provide remote pharmacy services at a remote healthcare site if a Class A or Class C pharmacy that dispenses prescription drug orders to outpatients is located in the same community (as defined in the rule).
Note: Community is defined by Board rule as within 10 miles if not in a metropolitan statistical area. This is applicable to telepharmacy systems in healthcare facilities or clinics. Remote dispensing sites have more restrictive rules (i.e., within 22 miles).
g. A provider pharmacy may not supervise more than 2 remote sites.
h. An application to TSBP is required before providing these services.
i. A perpetual inventory of all controlled substances must be maintained for each remote location. Each remote location's controlled substances must be inventoried on the same day as the provider pharmacy's inventory.
j. Original prescription records shall be kept at the remote site and the provider pharmacy shall have electronic access to those records.
k. The chart on the next page provides a summary and comparison of the two types of "remote sites" where telepharmacy is allowed.

Remote Healthcare Sites	Remote Dispensing Sites
Provider pharmacy may be a Class A or Class C pharmacy.	Provider pharmacy must be a Class A pharmacy.
Provider pharmacy may not supervise more than two remote sites.	Provider pharmacy may not supervise more than two remote sites.
No restriction on drug classes.	May not dispense Schedule II controlled substances.
Does not require a pharmacy technician.	Must be staffed by a pharmacy technician.
May not be located if a Class A or Class C pharmacy dispensing to outpatients is within 10 miles (if not located in a metropolitan statistical area).	May not be located if a Class A pharmacy is within 22 road miles.
A DEA Registration is required for controlled substances.	A DEA Registration is required for controlled substances.
Perpetual inventory of controlled substances is required.	Perpetual inventory of controlled substances is required.
No special training for pharmacy technicians (if used).	Pharmacy technicians must have one year of retail experience and training on a telepharmacy system.
No requirement for pharmacist visits or reconciliation of controlled substances.	Pharmacist employed by a provider pharmacy must make at least monthly onsite visits to a remote dispensing site and must reconcile the perpetual inventory of controlled substances to the on-hand count.
No limit on prescriptions dispensed.	If a remote dispensing site dispenses an average of more than 125 prescriptions each day the site is open (calculated annually), it must apply for a Class A license.

F. Destruction and Disposal of Dangerous Drugs and Controlled Substances (TSBP Rule Chapter 303 or TFPDL pages E.29-32) *Note: This process is not the same as a transfer of controlled substances to a DEA registered reverse distributor for destruction.*
   1. Destruction of Dispensed Drugs.
      a. Drugs Dispensed to Patients in Healthcare Facilities or Institutions (nursing homes).
         (1) Destruction of Dangerous Drugs by Consultant Pharmacist.
            (a) Inventory is required.
            (b) Drugs must be destroyed in a manner to render the drugs unfit for human consumption and disposed of in compliance with all applicable state and federal requirements.
            (c) Destruction is witnessed by a peace officer or agent of the Board, Texas Department of Human Services, or Texas Department of State Health Services, or 2 of the following persons from the facility: the facility administrator, the director of nursing, or a licensed nurse.
         (2) Destruction of Dangerous Drugs by a Waste Disposal Service.
            (a) Inventory is required.
            (b) Drugs are placed in a sealed container in presence of a witness (same list as in (1)(c) above).
            (c) Drugs must be destroyed in a manner to render the drugs unfit for human consumption and disposed of in compliance with all applicable state and federal requirements.
            (d) Waste disposal service provides the facility with proof of destruction of the sealed container.
         (3) Controlled Substances – Must follow DEA rules for destruction (*see Section Two of this Guide*).
      b. Drugs Returned to a Pharmacy.
         (1) Dangerous Drugs.
            (a) Drugs must be destroyed in a manner

to render the drugs unfit for human consumption and disposed of in compliance with all applicable state and federal requirements.
- (b) Document date of destruction, name and address of dispensing pharmacy, prescription number, name and strength of drug, and signature of pharmacist.
- (2) Controlled Substances – Pharmacy must be a collector under DEA destruction rules.

2. Destruction of Stock Drugs.
   a. Stock Dangerous Drugs.
      (1) Pharmacists licensed by the Texas State Board of Pharmacy may destroy stock dangerous drugs if the drugs are destroyed in a manner to render the drugs unfit for human consumption (i.e., destroyed beyond reclamation) and disposed of in compliance with all applicable state and federal requirements.
      (2) Records of destruction are not required.
   b. Stock Controlled Substances. *(See DEA destruction rules in Section Two of this Guide.)*

G. Other TSBP Rules
   1. Drug Recalls (TSBP Rule 291.7 or TFPDL page E.12). Requires the PIC to have policies and procedures for handling prescription drug recalls including ensuring that a recalled drug has been removed from inventory within 24 hours of notice of the recall.
   2. Return of Prescription Drugs (TSBP Rule 291.8 or TFPDL pages E.12-14). It is unlawful to accept prescription drugs that have been dispensed for purposes of resale. There is an exception for certain prescriptions dispensed to nursing home patients.
   Note: There is also a separate rule for returning undelivered prescriptions or prescriptions from a will call bin to stock. See Section Six, II. F.
   3. Prescription Pick Up Locations (TSBP Rule 291.9 or TFPDL page E.14).
      a. No person, firm, or business establishment may

participate in an arrangement whereby prescriptions are solicited, collected, picked up, or advertised to be picked up from any location other than a pharmacy licensed by the Board.
b. ==A pharmacy may, at the request of a patient, pick up prescription orders at the office or home of the prescriber, the residence or place of employment of the patient, or a hospital or medical care facility where the patient is receiving treatment.==
c. A pharmacy may deliver prescription drugs to the residence of a patient, the place of employment of a patient if the patient is present to accept delivery, a hospital or medical care facility in which the patient is receiving treatment, and the office of the prescriber for administration to the patient if the prescription is not for a controlled substance.
Note: TSBP modified this rule to not allow controlled substance prescriptions to be delivered to the prescriber's office to match DEA rules. However, the SUPPORT Act passed by Congress in late 2018 modified federal law to allow a pharmacy to deliver a controlled substance prescription to a practitioner if it is to be administered by injection or implant under certain conditions. TSBP may need to modify this rule to match the new federal law.

4. Pharmacy Balance Registration/Inspection (TSBP Rule 291.10 or TFPDL page E.14).
   a. Balance is required if a pharmacy performs nonsterile compounding.
   b. Balance must be registered with TSBP and shall be inspected for accuracy by the Board.
5. ==Pilot or Demonstration Projects (TSBP Rule 291.23 or TFPDL pages D.14-16). Specifies procedures to be followed to apply for approval of a research or demonstration project for innovative applications in the practice of pharmacy. TSBP may waive a rule to allow the pilot project but cannot waive a law.== *inter pharmacy transfers.*
6. Professional Responsibility of Pharmacists and the Practice of Telemedicine (TSBP Rule 291.29 or TFPDL pages E.20-21).
   a. Requires a pharmacist to exercise sound professional

judgment with respect to the accuracy and authenticity of any prescription dispensed and to verify the order if there are any questions.
   b. The rule expands the concept of a pharmacist's corresponding responsibility to ensure that controlled substances are issued for a legitimate medical purpose by a practitioner in the usual course of medical practice to all prescriptions including dangerous drugs and not just controlled substances.
   c. The rule indicates that a pharmacist may not dispense a prescription that was issued by means of the Internet unless it is pursuant to a valid prescription written for a legitimate medical purpose without at least one in-person medical examination. However, the practice of telemedicine is now legal in Texas, so prescriptions issued based on telephonic or Internet-based consultations are now allowed in Texas. *See TFPDL page D.82 and also Telemedicine Frequently Asked Questions on the TSBP website.*
   d. A pharmacist shall not dispense a prescription drug if the pharmacist knows or should know the prescription is fraudulent or forged. A pharmacist shall make every reasonable effort to prevent inappropriate dispensing due to fraudulent, forged, invalid, or medically inappropriate prescriptions. *See TSBP Rule 291.29 or TFPDL page E.21 (January 2019 Supplement) for a list of factors relevant to preventing nontherapeutic dispensing.*
7. Centralized Prescription Dispensing (TSBP Rule 291.125 or TFPDL pages E.21-22). Allows Class A or Class C pharmacies (the outsourcing pharmacy) to outsource prescription drug order dispensing to another Class A or C pharmacy or a Class E pharmacy (the central fill pharmacy) under certain conditions.
   a. Must be under common ownership or have written contract or agreement.
   b. Must share common database or have other technology to allow access to information.
   c. Must provide notice to patients (one time written notification) or a sign in the pharmacy.

    d. The prescription label should include the name of the outsourcing pharmacy and some unique identifier of the central fill pharmacy.
    e. DEA does not allow a central fill pharmacy to deliver controlled substance prescriptions directly to a patient, but TSBP does allow a central fill pharmacy to deliver dangerous drug prescriptions directly to a patient.
8. Centralized Prescription Drug or Medication Order Processing (TSBP Rule 291.123 or TFPDL pages E.22-23). Allows Class A, Class C, and Class E pharmacies to outsource prescription or medication order processing (data entry, drug regimen review, adjudication, etc.) to another Class A, C, or E pharmacy.
    a. Must be under common ownership or have written contract or agreement.
    b. Must share common database or have other technology to allow access to information.
    c. Must provide notice to patients of Class A and E pharmacies that Central Processing is being used to fill their prescriptions. One time notification or sign is required.
9. Satellite Pharmacy (TSBP Rule 291.129 or TFPDL pages E.23-29).
    a. This pharmacy is not what is typically considered to be a satellite pharmacy of a hospital pharmacy.
    b. This rule allows a Class A or C pharmacy to operate a satellite location that is not separately licensed.
    c. Prescriptions are dropped off at the satellite location and then sent to the Class A or C pharmacy to be filled. The filled prescriptions are then sent back to the satellite location where the patient picks up the prescription and counseling is provided as required.
    d. Detailed requirements can be found in TSBP Rule 291.129 or TFPDL pages E.23-29.
    e. This rule is an exception to the prohibition on prescription pick-up locations.
    f. No bulk prescription drugs are allowed to be stored in a satellite pharmacy.

Section Five

Complaints, Inspections, Disciplinary Actions, Penalties, and Procedures

Section Five

Complaints, Inspections, Disciplinary Actions, Penalties, and Procedures

I. **Notifications to the Public, Complaints, and Inspections**
   A. Notifications (TSBP Rule 291.3(h)(1) or TFPDL pages F.2-4)
      1. Pharmacies must post a sign notifying patients how they can file complaints with TSBP. Rule also allows for an electronic messaging system.
      2. If a pharmacy delivers prescriptions to patients, a written notification must be provided with the delivery.
      3. Pharmacies that maintain Internet sites must include general information on how to file a complaint on their initial home page where consumers can order refills and must provide specific information on how to file a complaint no more than 2 links away from the initial home page. Pharmacies whose Internet site is accredited by NABP's Verified Internet Pharmacy Practice Sites (VIPPS) or similar TSBP-approved programs are considered compliant with the notification requirements.
      4. Pharmacists not working in a pharmacy also must provide the notice to patients either posting a sign in the practice location or providing written notice to each patient when services are provided. *See TSBP Rule 295.11 or TFPDL pages F.3-4.*
   B. Complaints
      1. TSBP must adopt policies and procedures concerning the investigation of complaints filed with the Board.
      2. Confidentiality – The identity of any person who files a complaint with the Board is considered confidential information and is not subject to the Texas Open Records Act.
      3. Immunity – A person who files a complaint in good faith to the Board is immune from civil liability.
   C. Inspections and Investigations
      1. Before entering a facility for an inspection, the person authorized to represent the Board must state the purpose

for the inspection and provide the owner, pharmacist, or agent the appropriate credentials and a written notice of inspection authority.
2. A search warrant is not required.
3. The Board may inspect and copy documents; inspect a facility's storage, equipment, security, prescription drugs or devices, components used in compounding, finished and unfinished products, and records; and may perform an inventory and take samples of products.
4. The Board may inspect financial records only in relation to a specific complaint. Any financial data, sales data, or pricing data obtained by the Board during an inspection or investigation is confidential and not subject to the Texas Open Records Act.

> *Study Tip:* DEA does not have the authority to inspect financial, sales, or pricing records unless the pharmacy consents to the inspection.

5. Before filing a complaint for a violation as a result of a written warning notice issued during an inspection, TSBP must give the license holder a reasonable time to comply. TSBP considers a reasonable time to be no fewer than 10 days unless there is an imminent danger to the public health and safety.

II. Grounds for Discipline
A. Applicant for or Holder of a Pharmacist License (TPA Section 565.001)
   1. Violation of the TPA or any TSBP rule.
   2. Unprofessional Conduct. *(See TSBP Rule 281.7(a) or TFPDL pages F.10-13 for complete list.)*
      a. Dispensing fraudulent prescriptions or prescriptions based on orders not issued for a legitimate medical purpose.
      b. Delivering or offering to deliver a prescription drug in violation of law.
      c. Sharing or offering to share with a practitioner compensation received from an individual who was provided pharmacy services by a pharmacist.
      d. Refusing an inspection or failing to respond to a warning notice.

e. Engaging in conduct that subverts or attempts to subvert any examination (NAPLEX, MPJE) required for a license to practice pharmacy.
   f. Failing to practice pharmacy in an acceptable manner consistent with the public health and welfare.
   g. Obstructing a Board employee in the lawful performance of his or her duties.
   h. Failing to maintain effective controls to prevent the diversion or loss of controlled substances or dangerous drugs.
   i. ==Failing to repay a guaranteed student loan.==
   j. Failing to respond within the time specified on a warning notice issued as a result of a compliance inspection.
   k. Responding to an inspection warning notice in a manner that is false or misleading.
3. Gross Immorality (TSBP Rule 281.7(b) or TFPDL page F.13).
   a. ==Conduct which is willful, flagrant, and shameless and which shows moral indifference to community standards.==
   b. Engaging in an act which is a felony.
   c. Engaging in an act that constitutes sexually deviant behavior.
   d. Being required to register as a sex offender.
4. Incapacity.

Study Tip: Incapacity means that the practicing pharmacist has a mental or physical condition that may cause harm to the public if he or she continues to practice.

5. Fraud, Deceit, or Misrepresentation (TSBP Rule 281.7(c) or TFPDL page F.13).

Study Tip: One of the most common violations of this rule involves providing inaccurate information on an application for a license or renewal of a license.

6. Convicted or placed on deferred adjudication community supervision or deferred disposition or the applicable federal equivalent for a misdemeanor involving moral turpitude or a misdemeanor under the Texas Dangerous Drug Act, Texas or Federal Controlled Substances Act, or any felony.

7. Used alcohol or drugs in an intemperate manner.
8. Failed to keep and maintain records.
9. Violated the Controlled Substances Act or rules and Dangerous Drug Act or rules.
10. Aided or abetted an unlicensed individual to practice pharmacy.
11. Refused entry into a pharmacy for an authorized inspection.
12. Violated pharmacy or drug laws of this state or any other state.
13. Been negligent in the practice of pharmacy.
14. Failed to submit to mental or physical exam as required.
15. Dispensed prescription drugs outside the usual course of professional practice.
16. Been disciplined by the regulatory board of another state.
17. Violated a disciplinary order including a confidential order or contract under the program to aid impaired pharmacists and pharmacy students.
18. Failed to adequately supervise a task delegated to a pharmacy technician.
19. Inappropriately delegated a task to a pharmacy technician.
20. Been responsible for a drug audit shortage.
21. Been convicted or adjudicated of a criminal offense that requires registration as a sex offender.

B. Grounds for Discipline of Pharmacy Technicians and Pharmacy Technician Trainees (TSBP Rule 281.9 or TFPDL pages F.18-19)
1. The grounds for discipline of pharmacy technicians are substantially similar to the grounds for discipline of pharmacists.
2. An additional ground for discipline of pharmacy technicians is performing duties that only a pharmacist may perform.

C. Grounds for Discipline of an Applicant for or Holder of a Pharmacy License *(See TPA Section 565.002 or TFPDL pages F.14-17 for complete list.)*
1. Been convicted of or placed on deferred adjudication for a misdemeanor involving moral turpitude or a violation of the FCSA or any felony.
2. Advertised prescription drugs or devices in a deceitful, misleading, or fraudulent manner.

3. Sold prescription drugs without legal authorization.
4. Allowed an employee who is not a pharmacist to practice pharmacy.
5. Sold an adulterated or misbranded drug.
6. Failed to engage in the business described in the application for license within 6 months of the date of issuance of the license.
7. Ceased to engage in the business described in the application for a license for a period of 30 days or longer.

D. Grounds for Discipline of a Pharmacy License *(See TSBP Rule 281.8 or TFPDL pages F.16-17 for a complete list.)*
   1. Failed to establish and maintain adequate controls to prevent diversion of prescription drugs.
   2. Employed a pharmacist, intern, or pharmacy technician whose license has been revoked, cancelled, retired, surrendered, denied, or suspended.
   3. Possessed or engaged in the sale of prescription drug samples.
   4. Waived, discounted, or reduced a patient copay or deductible for a compounded drug in the absence of a legitimate documented financial hardship of the patient or evidence of a good faith effort to collect the copayment or deductible from the patient.

III. Penalties and Procedures (Applies to pharmacists, pharmacy technicians, and pharmacies)

A. Penalties (Discipline authorized)
   1. Reprimand – Public and formal censure of license.
   2. Restriction – Limit, confine, or restrain a license with certain terms or conditions.
   3. Suspension – License not in effect for specified amount of time.
   4. Probation – Placing a license under a period of supervision by the Board for a term and under conditions as determined by the Board, including a probation fee.
   5. Refuse to issue or renew a license.
   6. Revocation – License is void and no longer in effect.
   7. Retire – License is withdrawn and no longer in effect.
   8. Administrative Penalty – A fine; may be included with other sanctions above.

        a. Cannot exceed $5,000 per violation, but every day a violation occurs is a separate violation.
        b. Civil penalties for license violations and unlawful practice can be as much as $1,000 per day.
B. Rules of Procedure (How TSBP initiates formal disciplinary action against a licensee)
    1. Preliminary Notice Letter.
        a. When TSBP initiates disciplinary action against an applicant or licensee, it sends a Preliminary Notice Letter.
        b. If a Preliminary Notice letter is ignored, it could result in a default judgment against the license.
        c. The Preliminary Notice Letter will offer an opportunity to attend a non-public, informal conference.
        d. Most cases are voluntarily settled through the informal conference as described in 2. below. If a settlement cannot be reached through an informal process or if the licensee chooses not to go through the informal process, a formal conference is held as described in 3. below.
    2. Informal Conference (Non-public).
        a. This is a voluntary settlement conference where the licensee or applicant and/or his or her attorney meet with a TSBP panel consisting of one Board member, the Executive Director, and Director of Enforcement.
        b. TSBP is represented at the informal conference by the Board's general counsel.
        c. The Board's attorney presents the allegations from the Preliminary Notice Letter, and the licensee and/or his or her attorney are given an opportunity to show compliance with the law. If compliance with the law can be demonstrated, the charges will be dismissed.
        d. If the charges are not dismissed, the Board panel then deliberates and will make a recommendation to resolve the case by proposing an Agreed Board Order (ABO).
        e. The licensee can accept or reject the ABO. If it is accepted, it is presented to the full Board for approval. If it is rejected, the matter goes through the formal disciplinary process.
        f. Once an ABO has been approved, it cannot be appealed.

3. Formal Conference (Public hearing).
    a. A hearing (like a trial) is conducted in front of an Administrative Law Judge (ALJ).
    b. The ALJ issues findings of facts and conclusions of law and recommends sanctions to the Board in a Board Order (BO).
    c. The Board accepts, denies, or modifies the Board Order.
    d. A Board Order can be appealed to a Texas district court, but a motion for a rehearing must first be filed with TSBP.
4. Reissuance or Removal of Restriction on License. Before requesting the reissuing of a license that has been revoked or removing a restriction that has been placed on a license, the licensee must wait a minimum of 12 months.
5. Other Disciplinary Issues.
    a. Subpoena authority – The Board may issue subpoenas to compel attendance of witnesses or to compel the production of documents or records.
    b. Temporary suspension – A 3-member disciplinary panel appointed by the Board president may temporarily suspend or restrict a license if continued practice or operation of a pharmacy would constitute a continuing threat to the public welfare. A temporary suspension can take place immediately, without notice, if a hearing is scheduled not later than 14 days after the suspension or restriction.
    c. Remedial plan – The Board may enter into a remedial plan to resolve a complaint unless the complaint involves a death, hospitalization, commission of a felony, unlicensed practice, audit shortages, diversion of controlled substances, impairment, unauthorized dispensing, gross immorality, fraud, deceit, misrepresentation, or disciplinary action by a board of pharmacy in another state. Remedial plans are not considered formal disciplinary action but are public documents. Remedial plans are removed from a licensee's record after 5 years.

d. Alternative dispute resolution – The Board and a licensee can agree to mediate a disciplinary case through this process following an informal conference (when an agreement could not be reached) and before a formal disciplinary hearing is conducted.
e. Mental or physical exam – The Board may request or require an applicant, licensee, or registrant to submit to a mental or physical exam upon a finding of probable cause that identifies a mental or physical incapacity that would prevent him or her from practicing with a level of skill and competence that ensures the public health, safety, and welfare.

Section Six

Class A (Community) Pharmacy Rules

Section Six

Class A (Community) Pharmacy Rules

Note: All Class A pharmacies that compound sterile products must have a Class A-S license. This provides the Board the ability to identify which pharmacies are engaged in this activity. In addition to the sterile compounding rules, Class A-S pharmacies must also follow all rules for Class A pharmacies.

I. **Personnel**
   A. Pharmacist-in-Charge (PIC)
      1. Each Class A pharmacy shall have one PIC who is employed full time.
      2. Generally, the PIC may only be a PIC of one Class A pharmacy unless the additional Class A is not open at the same time. During an emergency, the PIC may serve as the PIC for 2 Class A pharmacies open at the same time if he or she works at least 10 hours per week in each pharmacy for no more than 30 consecutive days.
      3. Responsibilities of PIC.
         a. The legal operation of the pharmacy.
         b. Educating and training pharmacy technicians.
         See TSBP Rule 291.32 or TFPDL pages G.5-6 for complete list.
   B. Owner
      1. Has responsibility for all administrative and operational functions of the pharmacy.
      2. If not a pharmacist, must consult with the PIC or another pharmacist for establishing policies and procedures.
   C. Pharmacists
      1. Responsible for supervising pharmacy technicians and pharmacy technician trainees. Supervision may be done electronically if the pharmacist is on-site in the pharmacy and other conditions are met. *See TSBP Rule 291.32 or TFPDL pages G.6-8.*
      2. The dispensing pharmacist (defined as the pharmacist who performs the final check) is responsible for ensuring that drugs are dispensed safely and accurately as prescribed

unless the pharmacy's computer system can identify each pharmacist involved in different steps of the dispensing process such as drug regimen review, verification of data entry, labeling, etc.
3. Duties which may be performed only by a pharmacist:
   a. Receiving oral prescription drug orders and reducing these orders to writing.
   b. Interpreting prescription drug orders.
   c. Selecting drug products (means generic drug product selection).
   d. Performing the final check of a dispensed prescription.
   e. Patient counseling.
   f. Assuring that a reasonable effort is made to obtain, record, and maintain patient medication records.
   g. Interpreting patient medication records and performing drug regimen reviews.
   h. Performing drug therapy management under protocol.
   i. Verifying that controlled substances listed on invoices are received by initialing and dating invoices.
   j. Transferring or receiving a transfer of a prescription. Note: While most of these duties listed above may also be performed by an intern working under a preceptor, the transfer of a prescription requires at least one pharmacist to be involved. Transfers from an intern to a pharmacist or from a pharmacist to an intern are permitted, but transfers between two interns are not.

Study Tip: Be sure to know the duties that only a pharmacist (and an intern supervised by a preceptor) can perform, which are the duties a pharmacy technician cannot perform.

D. Pharmacy Technicians and Pharmacy Technician Trainees
   1. Individuals working in pharmacies whose responsibilities are to provide nonjudgmental, technical services associated with the dispensing of a prescription drug order.
   2. Duties may include:
      a. Initiating and receiving refill authorization requests.
      b. Initiating electronic transfer requests between pharmacies sharing a common database.
      c. Entering prescription data into a computer system.
      d. Taking a stock bottle from the shelf for a prescription.

  e. Preparing and packaging prescription drug orders.
  f. Affixing prescription labels and auxiliary labels to a prescription.
  g. Reconstituting medications.
  h. Loading bulk drugs into an automated counting or dispensing device provided a pharmacist verifies that the device is properly loaded prior to use.
  i. Loading prepackaged containers previously verified by a pharmacist or manufacturer's unit-of-use packages into an automated dispensing machine.
  j. Bulk compounding.
  k. Compounding nonsterile prescription drug orders after appropriate training.
  l. In a Class A-S pharmacy, compounding sterile preparations after appropriate training.

> **Study Tip:** *In a Class A pharmacy there are no differences between the duties of a pharmacy technician and a pharmacy technician trainee.*

  3. Ratio – The ratio of onsite pharmacists to technicians in a Class A pharmacy may be 1:4 if at least one of the technicians is a registered pharmacy technician. Otherwise, the ratio is 1:3.

II. Operational Standards
 A. Environment
  1. Orderly and clean.
  2. Sink with hot and cold running water, exclusive of restrooms.
  3. If serving the public, a patient counseling area shall be designed to maintain confidentiality.
  4. Appropriate lighting and temperature.
  5. No animals allowed.
  6. Designated area for flammable materials.

 B. Security (only applies to pharmacies that possess drugs)
  1. Prescription department must be locked by key, combination, or other mechanical or electronic means to prohibit unauthorized access.
  2. The pharmacy's key, combination, or means of locking the pharmacy may not be duplicated.
  3. At minimum, must have a basic alarm system with off-site monitoring and motion detectors.
  4. PIC or owner may authorize individuals to enter prescription

department to perform functions other than dispensing but must maintain written documentation of authorized individuals other than individuals employed by the pharmacy who access the prescription department when a pharmacist is not on-site.
5. Must have written policies and procedures for security.
C. Temporary Absence of a Pharmacist
Note: This rule applies when there is only one pharmacist on duty in the pharmacy.
1. Pharmacist Stays On-Site (for breaks and meals without closing prescription department) (TSBP Rule 291.33(b)(3)(A) or TFPDL pages G.14-15).
   a. At least one pharmacy technician (not a trainee) remains in the pharmacy.
   b. Pharmacist must remain on the premises of the facility.
   c. A notice must be posted that the pharmacist is on break.
   d. During a break, pharmacy technicians may begin processing prescription drug orders or refills, but those orders may not be delivered until the pharmacist returns and verifies the accuracy of the prescription. Upon return, the pharmacist must conduct a drug regimen review and verify all activities performed by the technician. Any pharmacist intern on duty may only act as a pharmacy technician while the pharmacist is absent.
   e. Patients may pick up prescriptions that have already been filled and checked by the pharmacist.

Study Tip: This section causes much confusion. How can a patient pick up a new prescription where counseling is required if the pharmacist is on break? The rules allow you to treat that prescription the same way you would treat a new prescription that is delivered to the patient at his or her home. Counseling is provided by giving written information about the drug and a notice that the patient can call the pharmacist if the patient has any questions. See explanation in TFPDL on page G.18.

2. Pharmacist is Off-Site (prescription department is closed) (TSBP Rule 291.33(b)(3)(B) or TFPDL pages G.15-16).
   a. If the pharmacist leaves the premises of the facility, the

prescription department must be closed, and pharmacy technicians may not remain in the pharmacy. However, this rule allows delivery of filled prescriptions under certain conditions after the pharmacy department has closed (as follows in b.).
b. During short periods of time when a pharmacist is absent from the pharmacy, an agent of the pharmacist may deliver a previously verified prescription (new or refill) to a patient in the pharmacy provided the short periods of time do not exceed 2 consecutive hours in a 24-hour period.

> ***Study Tip:*** *This is a rule very unique to Texas and allows filled prescriptions to be delivered to patients in the pharmacy for up to 2 hours after the pharmacy department is closed. It may be useful in locations such as grocery stores or other locations where the prescription department is closed but the rest of the store remains open.*

      c. The pharmacy must maintain a record of the date of delivery, prescription number, patient's name and phone number, and signature of person picking up the prescription.
      d. The pharmacy must also meet the same requirements of a prescription delivered to a patient at the patient's residence.
      e. The pharmacy may also use an automated storage and distribution device (kiosk) to deliver prescriptions. This is not restricted to the 2-hour limitation in b. above. (*See automation rules in J. of this section.*)
D. Patient Counseling and Drug Regimen Review
    1. Patient Counseling.
      a. Mandatory patient counseling is required for new prescription drug orders. *Note: New prescription drug orders include prescriptions that have not been dispensed to the patient by the pharmacy in the same strength and dosage form within the past year.*
      b. Information must be provided which, in the pharmacist's professional judgment, the pharmacist deems significant.

      c. Verbal and written information must be provided. Written information may be electronic (including email) if the patient has requested electronic communication and this request is documented.
      d. The pharmacy must document initials or identification code of the pharmacist providing counseling either on the prescription or in the computer system.
      e. If prescription is delivered to patient, must provide the following statement in English and Spanish: "Written information about this prescription has been provided for you. Please read this information before you take the medication. If you have any questions concerning this prescription, a pharmacist is available during normal business hours to answer those questions at (insert phone number)."
      f. Only a pharmacist may verbally provide drug information to a patient and answer questions concerning prescription drugs. Non-pharmacist personnel and/or the pharmacy's computer system may not ask questions of a patient which are intended to screen or limit interaction with the pharmacist.

> **Study Tip:** While a patient may refuse counseling, there is no such thing as an "offer to counsel" in Texas. Counseling is required for all new prescription drug orders. Any refusal of counseling by a patient or patient's agent must be documented.

2. Drug Regimen Review.
      a. Required for all prescriptions (new and refill).
      b. At a minimum, the pharmacist shall review and identify clinically significant:
          (1) Known allergies.
          (2) Rational drug therapy/contraindications.
          (3) Reasonable dose and route of administration.
          (4) Reasonable directions for use.
          (5) Duplication of therapy.
          (6) Drug-drug interactions.
          (7) Drug-food interactions.
          (8) Drug-disease interactions.
          (9) Adverse drug reactions.
          (10) Proper utilization, including overutilization and underutilization.

E. **Labeling Requirements for Dispensed Prescriptions**
   1. Name, address, and phone number of the pharmacy.
   2. Prescription number (easily readable font no smaller than 10-point Times Roman).
   3. Date dispensed.
   4. Initials or identification code of the dispensing pharmacist (not required if maintained in computer system).
   5. Name of prescriber.
   6. Name of pharmacist signing a prescription drug order (if applicable).
   7. Name of patient. If for an animal, the species of the animal and name of owner.
   8. Instructions for use (easily readable font no smaller than 10-point Times Roman).
   9. Quantity dispensed.
   10. Appropriate ancillary instructions.
   11. If for a Schedule II-IV drug, the federal transfer statement "Caution: Federal law prohibits the transfer of this drug to any person other than the patient for whom it was prescribed."

Study Tip: *The federal transfer caution is not required for Schedule V drugs or dangerous drugs even though many pharmacies comply by preprinting it on every label.*

   12. "Substituted for Brand Prescribed" or "Substituted for 'Brand Name'" if generic substitution has occurred.
   13. Name and strength of drug dispensed unless otherwise directed by prescriber (easily readable font no smaller than 10-point Times Roman).
   14. A beyond-use date that is not greater than one year from date dispensed or manufacturer's expiration date whichever is shorter.
   15. Either the prescription label or the written information accompanying the prescription shall contain the statement "Do not flush unused medications or pour down a sink or drain." A drug product on a list of medicines developed by the Federal Food and Drug Administration recommended for disposal by flushing is not required to bear this statement.

Note: The labeling requirements 1-15 above are not required to be met if the drug is for administration to an ultimate user who is institutionalized (hospital or nursing home patient) and not more than a 90-day supply is dispensed at one time. See TSBP Rule 291.33(c)(7)(D) or TFPDL pages G.23-24.

> **Study Tip:** *Although you rely on your computer system to print prescription labels, it is important to know the required elements on a label.*

- F. Returning Undelivered Medication to Stock
    1. Prescriptions that have not been picked up or delivered may be returned to pharmacy's stock for dispensing.
    2. Pharmacist must evaluate quality and safety of the prescriptions.
    3. Prescriptions cannot be mixed in with manufacturer's containers and must be placed in a new container when dispensed (with some exceptions).
- G. Equipment and Supplies
    1. Data processing system (computer) including a printer.
    2. Refrigerator.
    3. Child-resistant, light-resistant, and, if applicable, glass-tight containers.
    4. Prescription, poison, and other applicable labels.
    5. Metric/apothecary weight and measure conversion charts.
    6. Class A prescription balance if the pharmacy compounds prescription drug orders.
- H. Library (May be hard copy or electronic)
    1. Laws and rules – Texas Pharmacy Act, Texas Dangerous Drug Act, Texas Controlled Substances Act, and Federal Controlled Substances Act and rules.
    2. At least one current general drug information reference which includes drug interaction information.
    3. If the pharmacy dispenses veterinary prescriptions, a general reference on veterinary drugs.
    4. Basic antidote information and phone number of the nearest Regional Poison Control Center.
- I. Customized Patient Medication Packages (Med Paks)
    1. A pharmacist may, with consent of the patient or the prescriber, provide a customized patient med pak, which is a container holding 2 or more prescribed solid oral dosage

forms. The med pak container is designed so that each drug is labeled with the day and/or time each drug is to be taken.
2. ==Must have a prescription number for the med pak and a separate prescription number for each of the drugs within.==
3. Must have a beyond-use date not exceeding one year from the date dispensed or the earliest manufacturer's expiration date for a drug in the med pak.

J. Automated Devices and Systems – There are 4 types of automated devices and systems.
1. Automated Compounding or Counting Devices.
   a. Must be calibrated and verified on a routine basis.
   b. Records of loading the device must be maintained.
   c. Pharmacist must verify and sign that system is properly loaded prior to use.
2. Automated Pharmacy Dispensing System.
   a. System must have been tested and found to dispense accurately.
   b. Must operate according to a written quality assurance program which requires continuous monitoring and tests accuracy at least every 6 months or when an upgrade or change is made to the system.
   c. Must operate under written policies and procedures.
   d. Must have a recovery plan for disasters or other interruptions.
   e. System may be stocked or loaded by a pharmacist or a pharmacy technician or trainee under the supervision of a pharmacist.
   f. Final check may be accomplished by:
      1) A pharmacist checking the final product after the automated system has completed the prescription and prior to delivery to the patient or
      (2) A pharmacist verifying that any bulk stock drugs have been accurately stocked and the pharmacist checks the accuracy of the data entry of each prescription entered into the system.
      Note: Because this method does not require a pharmacist to check the bottle or the label at the end of the process, it requires that the system be fully automated from the time the pharmacist releases the prescription to the system until a completed, labeled prescription ready for delivery is produced.

3. **Automated Storage and Distribution Device (prescription pick-up kiosk).** A pharmacy may use an automated storage and distribution device to deliver a previously verified prescription to a patient or patient's agent when the pharmacy is open or when it is closed provided:
   a. The pharmacist-in-charge is responsible for the supervision of the system.
   b. The patient is counseled via a direct telephone link by a Texas-licensed pharmacist.
   c. Drugs are stored at proper temperatures.
   d. The patient or patient's agent is given the option to use the system.
   e. The automated storage and distribution device has been tested by the pharmacy and found to dispense prescriptions accurately.
   f. The automated storage and distribution device may be loaded with previously verified prescriptions only by a pharmacist or by pharmacy technicians under the direction and direct supervision of a pharmacist.
   g. The pharmacy will make the automated storage and distribution device and any testing records available for inspection by the Board.
   h. The automated storage and distribution device has an adequate security system, including security cameras, to prevent unauthorized access and to maintain patient confidentiality.
   i. The automated storage and distribution device records a digital image of the individual accessing the device to pick up a prescription, and such record is maintained by the pharmacy for 2 years.
   j. If an automated storage and delivery system is located at a remote delivery site (not in a pharmacy), the remote pharmacy services rule (291.121(d)) must be followed, including a requirement that the remote delivery site is approved by TSBP.

Study Tip: Previously, automated storage and delivery systems (kiosks) were only permitted to be located in a pharmacy, were only allowed to be used for refills of prescriptions, and could not be used for controlled substances. However, TSBP updated this rule in 2018 to eliminate those restrictions.

4. Automated Checking Device. A fully automated device which confirms, after dispensing but prior to delivery to the patient, that the correct drug and drug strength have been labeled with the correct label for the correct patient.

> *Study Tip:* An automated checking device and automated pharmacy system both can be used to complete the final check of a prescription, but in an automated pharmacy dispensing system, the system is actually filling the prescription while checking for accuracy. With an automated checking device, prescriptions are checked for accuracy after dispensing using technology such as barcoding.

III. Records
  A. General Rules
   1. All records shall be maintained for 2 years.
   2. Schedule II records shall be maintained separately from other records.
   3. Schedule III-V records, other than prescriptions, shall be maintained separately or be "readily retrievable" from other records. "Readily retrievable" means that the controlled substance records are asterisked, redlined, or in some other manner readily identifiable from other items in the record. Note: Although Texas law allows imaging of original records for Schedule II-V controlled substances, DEA requires the hardcopy original records be kept for 2 years.
  B. Patient Medication Records (Required for all new patients)
   1. Must provide for the immediate retrieval of information for the previous 12 months to conduct a drug regimen review.
   2. PIC must assure that a reasonable effort is made to obtain and record at least the following information:
      a. Name, address, and telephone number of patient.
      b. Age and gender of patient.
      c. Known allergies, drug reactions, idiosyncrasies, and chronic conditions or disease states.
      d. Other drugs currently being used by the patient.
      e. Pharmacist's comments relevant to drug therapy.
      f. A list of all prescription drug orders dispensed (new and refill) to the patient by the pharmacy during the last 2 years.

C. Computer System
   1. System must be backed up at least monthly.
   2. Must maintain any information (records) purged from computer for 2 years from the date of final entry of data.
   3. Must have capacity to produce a daily hardcopy printout consisting of:
      a. Prescription number.
      b. Date of dispensing.
      c. Patient name.
      d. Prescriber's name.
      e. Name and strength of the drug dispensed.
      f. Quantity dispensed.
      g. Initials or identification code of the dispensing pharmacist.
      h. Initials or identification code of pharmacy technician performing data entry, if applicable.
      i. If not immediately retrievable, must also include patient's address, prescriber's address, prescriber's DEA number if a controlled substance, quantity dispensed if different from quantity prescribed, date of issuance of prescription (if different from date of dispensing), and total refills dispensed to date.
      j. Any changes made to a record of dispensing.
   4. Daily hardcopy printout shall be produced within 72 hours of the date the prescriptions were dispensed.
   5. Each pharmacist who dispensed or refilled a prescription shall verify that the information is correct by signing and dating the hardcopy printout within 7 days from the date of dispensing.
   6. Pharmacy may maintain a daily logbook that pharmacists may sign daily in lieu of the daily hardcopy printout in 3. above, but the computer system must be able to produce an "audit trail" consisting of 3.(a.-j.) above within 72 hours.
   7. Each time a modification, change, or manipulation is made to a record of dispensing, documentation of such change shall be recorded in the computer system. The documentation of any modification, change, or manipulation to a record of dispensing shall include the identification of the individual responsible for the alteration.

8. Pharmacies must maintain a log of the unique initials or identification codes which will identify each pharmacist, pharmacy technician, and pharmacy technician trainee who is involved in the dispensing process in the pharmacy's data processing system. The initials or identification code shall be unique to ensure that each individual can be identified (i.e., identical initials or identification code shall not be used). This log shall be maintained at the pharmacy for at least 7 years from the date of the transaction.

> **Study Tip:** This is the only TSBP rule that requires a record be kept for 7 years.

D. Transfer of Prescription Drug Order Information
   1. Transfers must be communicated verbally or via fax directly between pharmacists or from a pharmacist to an intern. *Note: Transfer between 2 interns is not permitted.*
   2. Transfers may also be conducted electronically as long as specific requirements are met.
   3. Transfers of controlled substance prescriptions are allowed only one time unless the pharmacies share an electronic, real-time database.
   4. DEA and TSBP do not generally permit a pharmacy to transfer a controlled substance prescription that has been received at a pharmacy but not yet filled to another pharmacy. *Note: By policy DEA does allow this if the original prescription was transmitted electronically and it can be transferred electronically. However, TSBP rules or policy do not allow for this exception.*
   5. The prescription that is transferred must be voided in the computer system (or by writing "void" across the prescription if using a manual recordkeeping system).
   6. An individual may not refuse to transfer a prescription, and transfers must be completed within 4 business hours of a request.
   7. The electronic transfer of multiple or bulk prescription transfers is permitted.

Section Seven

Other Classes of Pharmacies

Section Seven

Other Classes of Pharmacies

I. **Class C (Institutional) Pharmacy Rules**
   A. Personnel
      1. Requirements for Pharmacist Services.
         a. A facility with 101 beds or more shall be under the continuous on-site supervision of a pharmacist when the pharmacy department is open for services.
         b. A facility with 100 beds or fewer shall have the services of a pharmacist at least part time or on a consulting basis, but the pharmacist must be on-site at least once every 7 days.
         c. If an institution operates an outpatient pharmacy, there must be a pharmacist on-site when the outpatient pharmacy is open. The outpatient pharmacy must also meet all Class A rules, including the pharmacy technician to pharmacist ratio.
      2. Pharmacist-in-Charge (PIC).
         a. A pharmacist must be accessible in all Class C pharmacies at all times although this may be provided through a telephone service that is answered 24 hours a day, a paging service, or a list of phone numbers where a pharmacist may be reached.
         b. Facilities with 101 beds or more must have one full-time PIC who can only be PIC for one such facility. This PIC may not serve as a PIC for a Class A or B pharmacy.
         c. Facilities with 100 beds or fewer must have a PIC who may be employed or under contract as a consultant and may be part time. One pharmacist may be PIC of no more than 3 such facilities or 150 beds. A pharmacist may be the PIC of one facility with 101 beds or more and one facility with 100 beds or fewer as long as the total number of beds does not exceed 150.
         d. PIC responsibilities.
            (1) Assuring the legal operation of the pharmacy.

(2) Providing appropriate level of pharmaceutical care services.
(3) Ensuring drugs and/or devices are prepared and distributed safely and accurately as prescribed.
(4) Participating in development of a formulary for the facility.
(5) Supervising a system to ensure maintenance of effective controls against prescription drug diversion. *See complete list in TSBP Rule 291.73(b)(2) or TFPDL pages I.5-6.*

3. Pharmacists.
   a. Responsible for delegated acts performed by pharmacy technicians and pharmacy technician trainees.
   b. The distributing pharmacist (defined as the pharmacist who checks the medication prior to distribution) is responsible for ensuring that the drug is prepared for distribution safely and accurately as prescribed, unless the pharmacy's computer system can record and identify each pharmacist involved in the preparation process. This includes drug regimen review, verification of data entry, preparation, distribution, and labeling.

4. Pharmacy Technicians.
   a. In facilities with 101 beds or more, the following duties may be performed under physically present pharmacist supervision:
      (1) Prepackaging and labeling unit-dose and multiple-dose packages.
      (2) Preparing, packaging, compounding, or labeling prescription drugs pursuant to medication orders.
      (3) Compounding nonsterile pharmaceuticals after appropriate training.
      (4) Compounding sterile pharmaceuticals after appropriate training (Class A-S only).
      (5) Bulk compounding or batch preparation.
      (6) Distributing routine orders for stock supplies to patient care areas.
      (7) Entering medication orders and drug distribution information into a computer system.
      (8) Loading unlabeled drugs into an automated compounding or counting device.

    (9) Accessing automated medication supply systems.
  b. In facilities with 100 beds or fewer, the following duties may be performed under physically present pharmacist supervision:
    (1) Prepackaging and labeling unit-dose and multiple-dose packages.
    (2) Bulk compounding or batch preparation.
    (3) Loading unlabeled drugs into an automated compounding or drug dispensing system.
    (4) Compounding medium-risk and high-risk sterile preparations after appropriate training (Class C-S only).
  c. In facilities with 100 beds or fewer, the following duties must be performed under the physically present or electronic supervision of a pharmacist:
    (1) Preparing, packaging, compounding, or labeling prescription drugs pursuant to medication orders.
    (2) Distributing routine orders for stock supplies to patient care areas.
    (3) Entering medication orders and drug distribution information into a computer system.
    (4) Accessing automated supply systems.
    (5) Compounding nonsterile preparations.
    (6) Compounding low-risk sterile preparations after appropriate training (Class C-S only).
  d. Ratio – There is no ratio of pharmacists to technicians in a Class C pharmacy.
  e. Special rules apply to rural hospitals. See B. below.
  f. Tech-Check-Tech – A Class C pharmacy that has an on-going clinical pharmacy program may allow a technician (not a technician trainee) to verify the work of another technician (not a technician trainee) relating to the filling of floor stock and unit-dose distribution systems if the patient's orders have been previously reviewed by a pharmacist. See TPA Section 568.008 or TFPDL page I.10.
B. Rural Hospitals (75 beds or fewer and located in a county with a population fewer than 50,000 or designated as a critical access hospital, rural referral center, or sole community hospital)
  1. If a practitioner orders a prescription drug or device

for a patient in a rural hospital when the pharmacist is not on duty or when the pharmacy is closed, a nurse or practitioner may withdraw the drug from the pharmacy in sufficient quantity to fulfill the order.
   2. The hospital pharmacist must verify the withdrawal and perform a drug regimen review no later than 7 days after the withdrawal.
   3. In a rural hospital, pharmacy technicians, but not trainees, may perform the following duties without direct supervision of a pharmacist:
      a. Entering medication orders and drug distribution information into a computer system.
      b. Preparing, packaging, or labeling prescription drugs pursuant to medication orders if a licensed nurse practitioner or pharmacist verifies the accuracy by electronic supervision before administration to the patient.
      c. Filling medication carts used in the rural hospital.
      d. Distributing routine orders for stock supplies to patient care areas.
      e. Accessing and restocking automated medication supply cabinets.

      Note: A nurse or practitioner at the hospital or a pharmacist through electronic supervision must verify the accuracy of the pharmacy technician performing these duties.

C. Absence of a Pharmacist
   1. In facilities with a full-time pharmacist when the pharmacy is closed:
      a. A designated licensed nurse or practitioner may remove drugs for the patient's immediate therapeutic needs.
      b. A record of the withdrawal must be made containing:
         (1) Name of patient.
         (2) Name, strength, and dosage form of device or drug.
         (3) Dose prescribed.
         (4) Quantity taken.
         (5) Time and date taken.
         (6) Signature.
      c. A pharmacist must verify withdrawal as soon as possible but no more than 72 hours after withdrawal.
   2. In facilities with a part-time or consultant pharmacist when the pharmacy is closed:

       a. A designated licensed nurse or practitioner may remove drugs and devices for the patient's immediate therapeutic needs.
       b. A pharmacist shall verify the withdrawal of the drugs from the pharmacy after a reasonable interval but in no event may the interval exceed 7 days.
       c. The pharmacist shall perform a drug regimen review within 96 hours if the facility has an average daily census above 10 and within 7 days if the facility has an average daily census of 10 or fewer.
       d. If using a floor stock system of distribution, the same rules apply and the pharmacist must verify withdrawal no later than 7 days after withdrawal.
- D. Library Requirements (either electronic or hard copy)
    1. Current copies of Texas Pharmacy Act, Texas Dangerous Drug Act, Texas Controlled Substances Act, and Federal Controlled Substances Act and rules.
    2. Drug interaction reference.
    3. General drug information reference.
    4. Injectable drug products reference.
    5. Basic antidote information and phone number of the nearest Poison Control Center.
    6. Metric/apothecary weight and measure conversion chart.
- E. Operational Standards
    1. Formulary is required.
    2. Prepackaging of drugs is allowed for distribution within the facility or for distribution to other Class C pharmacies under common ownership. Specific recordkeeping requirements must be met.
    3. Written policies and procedures of a drug distribution system are required. *See TSBP Rule 291.74(f)(5)(B) or TFPDL pages I.21-23 for detailed requirements.*
    4. Drug regimen review must be conducted on a prospective basis when a pharmacist is on duty and on a retrospective basis when a pharmacist is not on duty. The retrospective review must be conducted within 72 hours if the hospital has a full-time pharmacist. If the hospital has a part-time pharmacist, the drug regimen review must be conducted within 96 hours if the facility has an average daily census above 10 and within 7 days if the facility has an average daily census of 10 or fewer.

5. Floor stock records must be reviewed by a pharmacist at least every 30 days.
6. A perpetual inventory of Schedule II controlled substances is required.

F. Emergency Rooms
   1. When a pharmacist is on duty in the facility, any drugs dispensed for outpatient use including to emergency room patients must be dispensed by a pharmacist.
   2. When a pharmacist is not on duty, dangerous drugs and controlled substances may be supplied to patients admitted to the emergency room under the following conditions:
      a. Only drugs on an emergency room drug list may be provided.
      b. Drugs are supplied in prepackaged quantities not to exceed a 72-hour supply.
      c. Drugs are prepackaged by the pharmacy department, and at time of delivery the label is completed by the practitioner or nurse with:
         (1) Name, address, and telephone number of the facility.
         (2) Date supplied.
         (3) Name of practitioner.
         (4) Name of patient.
         (5) Directions for use.
         (6) Unique identification number (prescription number).
         (7) Brand name or generic name and strength of the drug used.
         (8) Quantity supplied.
      d. Pharmacist shall verify the contents of the emergency room drug list records at least once every 7 days.

G. Automated Devices and Systems
   1. Automated Compounding or Counting Devices.
      a. Must be calibrated and tested for accuracy.
      b. May be loaded by a pharmacy technician but must be verified by a pharmacist prior to use.
   2. Automated Medication Supply Systems.
      a. Include robotic systems and nursing unit-based storage systems such as Pyxis®.
      b. Must be tested and verified for accuracy.

- c. Must operate according to a written quality assurance program which requires continuous monitoring and tests accuracy at least every 6 months or when an upgrade or change is made to the system.
- d. Must operate under written policies and procedures.
- e. May be restocked by a pharmacy technician provided the medication has been checked by a pharmacist prior to restocking or system uses machine-readable product identifiers such as bar codes.
- f. Pharmacy must have a written plan for recovery from a disaster or other situation that disrupts the automated system.

H. Records
1. All records must be maintained for 2 years and must be supplied within 72 hours upon request.
2. Schedule II records must be maintained separately from other records.
3. Schedule III-V records must be maintained separately or be "readily retrievable."
4. Outpatient pharmacy records must be maintained under Class A rules.
5. Patient medication records must be maintained for each patient.
6. Computer system must be able to produce a hardcopy printout of an audit trail of all drugs distributed in the facility including specific information such as patient's name and room number or identification number; prescribing physician; drug name, strength, and dosage form; and quantity. Any audit trail requested must be provided within 72 hours.

I. Class C Pharmacies in a Freestanding Ambulatory Surgical Center (C-ASC)
1. If the facility has a full-time pharmacist, drugs withdrawn from a Class C-ASC pharmacy must be reviewed by a pharmacist within 72 hours.
2. If the facility has a part-time or consultant pharmacist, the pharmacist must conduct an audit of patient charts according to the schedule set out in the pharmacy's policy and procedure manual, but it must be at least once every calendar week the pharmacy is open.

3. Class C-ASC pharmacies must maintain a perpetual inventory of all controlled substances.
4. Invoices of dangerous drugs and controlled substances in a Class C-ASC pharmacy must be dated and initialed by the person receiving the drugs, and a pharmacist must verify that the controlled substances were entered into the perpetual inventory with his or her initials.
5. A pharmacist must conduct an audit by randomly comparing the distribution records with the medication orders at least every 30 days.
6. Postoperative drugs may only be supplied to patients admitted to the ASC from the approved drug list.
7. Drugs may only be supplied in prepackaged quantities not to exceed a 72-hour supply.

II. Class B (Nuclear) Pharmacy Rules
   A. Also regulated by the Texas Department of State Health Services through their Radiation Control Program (Radioactive Material License).
   B. Authorized Nuclear Pharmacists
      1. Must be a Board of Pharmaceutical Specialties (BPS) Certified Nuclear Pharmacist or
      2. Must complete 700 hours of a structured education program:
         a. 200 hours of didactic training approved by the TDSHS Radiation Control Program.
         b. 500 hours of supervised experience.
   C. Nuclear Pharmacist to Pharmacy Technician Ratio – Not more than 1:4 provided at least one is a registered pharmacy technician and not a pharmacy technician trainee.
   D. Policy and procedure manual is required.
   E. Federal Department of Transportation (DOT) regulations must be met.
   F. Outer Container Labeling Requirement
      1. Name, address, and phone number of the pharmacy.
      2. Date dispensed.
      3. Directions for use.
      4. Prescription number.
      5. Name of the patient, if known, or "for physician use" if the name of the patient is not known.
      6. Radiation symbol.

7. The words "Caution - Radioactive Material" or "Danger - Radioactive Material."
8. The name of the radiopharmaceutical or its abbreviation.
9. Amount of radioactivity in millicuries or microcuries or bequerels and the corresponding time that applies to this activity if different from the requested calibration date and time.
10. Initials or identification code of the person preparing and the nuclear pharmacist checking the product.
11. If a liquid, volume in milliliters.
12. Requested calibration date and time.
13. Expiration date and time.

G. Inner Container Label
1. Standard radiation symbol.
2. "Caution - Radioactive Material" or "Danger - Radioactive Material."
3. Name of radiopharmaceutical or its abbreviation.
4. Prescription number.

H. Refills – Refills of radioactive prescriptions are not allowed.
I. Preparation of sterile radiopharmaceuticals must meet requirements of sterile compounding rules which contain special exemptions and exceptions for certain provisions that cannot be met in nuclear pharmacies.

III. Class D (Clinic) Pharmacy Rules
A. Definitions and Personnel
1. Clinic – A facility/location other than a physician's office where limited types of dangerous drugs or devices restricted to those listed in and approved for the clinic's formulary are stored, administered, provided, or dispensed only to outpatients of the clinic.
2. License – A copy of the Class D pharmacy's policy and procedure manual and formulary is required as part of the license application.
3. Pharmacist-in-Charge.
   a. Employed or under written agreement as a consultant to the facility.
   b. May be the PIC for any number of clinics.
   c. Responsibilities include:
      (1) Continuous supervision (not on-site) of nurses, physician assistants, and others carrying out pharmacy-related aspects of the provision of drugs.

   (2) Documented on-site visits.
   (3) Development of a formulary.
  See TSBP Rule 291.92 or TFPDL page J.11 for complete list.
 4. Supportive Personnel – Responsible for provision of drugs according to written policies and procedures and completion of the drug label.

B. Formulary
 1. May include:
  a. Anti-infective drugs.
  b. Musculoskeletal drugs.
  c. Vitamins.
  d. Obstetrical and gynecological drugs.
  e. Topical drugs.
  f. Serums, toxoids, and vaccines.
 2. May not include:
  a. Nalbuphine (Nubain®).
  b. Drugs to treat erectile dysfunction.
  c. Controlled substances.

C. Expanded Formulary
 1. May petition TSBP for an expanded formulary if serving at least 80% indigent patients.
 2. An expanded formulary may provide for other drugs based upon the documented objectives of the clinic but not those listed in B.2. above.
 3. Additional requirements if using an expanded formulary:
  a. Supportive personnel providing drugs must be licensed nurses or practitioners.
  b. Must have policies and procedures for drugs on the formulary that require special monitoring.
  c. Retrospective drug regimen reviews of a random sample of clinic patients must be done on a quarterly basis.
  d. If the pharmacy provides antipsychotic drugs, the therapy must be initiated by a physician of the clinic. A practitioner shall monitor ongoing therapy, and the patient shall be physically examined by a physician at least yearly.

D. Provision of Drugs
 1. Drugs are prepackaged and labeled with the name and address of the clinic, name and strength of the drug, quantity, lot number and expiration date, directions for use (may be incomplete), and appropriate ancillary labels.

2. Drugs are provided to patients by designated supportive personnel who complete the label with the patient's name, any information necessary to complete directions for use, date of provision, and practitioner's name.
3. Patient counseling shall be provided at the time of provision.
4. If using an expanded formulary, only licensed nurses or physician assistants may provide drugs.
5. A Class D pharmacy may store and provide samples of dangerous drugs on the clinic's formulary that have been supplied to the clinic's practitioners from a manufacturer.

E. Dispensing of Drugs
Dangerous drugs may only be dispensed by a pharmacist in a Class D pharmacy pursuant to a prescription drug order.

> *Study Tip:* Be sure you understand the difference between the dispensing of dangerous drugs and the provision of dangerous drugs in a Class D pharmacy.

F. Supervision
1. PIC, consultant pharmacist, or staff pharmacist must personally visit the clinic at least monthly.
2. Clinics operated by state or local governments or funded by government sources may petition TSBP for an alternative visitation schedule.

IV. Class E (Nonresident) Pharmacy Rules

A. Class E pharmacies are nonresident (not located in Texas) pharmacies whose primary business is to dispense a prescription drug or device under a prescription drug order and deliver the drug or device to patients in Texas.

> *Study Tip:* A mail order pharmacy that is located in Texas would not have a Class E license. It would have a Class A license. Class E licenses are only issued to out-of-state pharmacies.

B. Pharmacies must have a license in good standing in their home state.
C. Individual pharmacists working in the pharmacy do not have to have a Texas license, but the PIC of a Class E pharmacy must be a Texas licensed pharmacist.

- D. Pharmacies must be able to provide dispensing records within 72 hours of TSBP request.
- E. Unless compliance would violate the pharmacy or drug laws or rules in the state in which the pharmacy is located, Class E pharmacies are required to comply with the provisions of TSBP Rules 291.101-291.105 relating to purpose, definitions, personnel, operational standards, and records.
- F. Patient counseling is required for all new prescription drug orders. Since prescriptions filled by Class E pharmacies are mailed to patients, they are treated as delivered prescriptions. A Class E pharmacy may meet the counseling requirements by providing written information regarding the prescription drug, along with a statement that a pharmacist is available via a toll-free telephone number for counseling.
- G. A Class E pharmacy that compounds sterile products must register with TSBP as a Class E-S pharmacy.

V. **Class F (Freestanding Emergency Medical Care Facility) Pharmacy Rules**
   - A. Definitions and Personnel
     1. A Freestanding Emergency Medical Care Facility (FEMCF) is a freestanding facility that is licensed by the Texas Department of State Health Services to provide emergency care to patients.
     2. An FEMCF must have one pharmacist-in-charge who is employed or contracted at least on a consulting or part-time basis.
   - B. Operational Standards
     1. The pharmacy and storage area for prescription drugs must be enclosed and capable of being locked.
     2. Only individuals authorized by the PIC may enter the pharmacy or have access to storage areas for prescription drugs.
     3. The pharmacy shall have locked storage for Schedule II controlled substances.
     4. In the absence of a pharmacist, only a designated licensed nurse or practitioner may remove drugs from the pharmacy in sufficient quantities for the immediate therapeutic needs of a patient.
     5. In Class F pharmacies with a full-time pharmacist, the

pharmacist shall verify the withdrawal of drugs from the pharmacy as soon as practical but no more than 72 hours from the time of such withdrawal.
6. In Class F pharmacies with a part-time or consultant pharmacist, the pharmacist shall conduct an audit of patient charts according to the schedule set out in the policy and procedures manual at least once in every calendar week that the pharmacy is open.
7. A Class F pharmacy must maintain a perpetual inventory of all controlled substances which shall be verified for completeness and reconciled at least once in every calendar week that the pharmacy is open.
8. Invoices of dangerous drugs and controlled substances must be dated and initialed or signed by the person receiving the drugs. A pharmacist shall verify that the controlled drugs listed on the invoices were added to the pharmacy's perpetual inventory by clearly recording his or her initials and the date of review of the perpetual inventory.
9. Drugs on an approved outpatient drug list may be supplied for outpatient use only in prepackaged quantities not to exceed a 72-hour supply if prelabeled by the pharmacy. At the time of delivery of the drug, the practitioner or licensed nurse under the practitioner's supervision must complete the label.
10. A retrospective random drug regimen review must be conducted at least every 31 days to verify proper usage of drugs.

VI. **Class G (Central Prescription Drug Order or Medication Order Processing) Pharmacy Rules**
   A. A Class G pharmacy license is issued to a facility established for the primary purpose of processing prescription drug or medication drug orders on behalf of another pharmacy, a healthcare provider, or a payor.
   B. A Class G pharmacy does not possess, store, or dispense drugs but may perform the following:
      1. Receiving, interpreting, or clarifying prescription drug or medication drug orders.
      2. Data entering and transferring of prescription drug or medication order information.

3. Performing drug regimen review.
4. Obtaining refill and substitution authorizations.
5. Verifying accurate prescription data entry.
6. Interpreting clinical data for prior authorization for dispensing.
7. Performing therapeutic interventions.
8. Providing drug information concerning a patient's prescription.

C. A Class G pharmacy may have a ratio of pharmacists to pharmacy technicians and pharmacy technician trainees of 1:8. However, only one of those may be a technician trainee.

VII. Class H (Limited Prescription Delivery) Pharmacy Rules

A. A Class H pharmacy has a unique and limited type of pharmacy license. It is owned by a hospital district and is located in a county without another pharmacy.
B. A Class H pharmacy provides limited prescription services for a Class A pharmacy operated by the hospital district.
C. A Class H pharmacy shall not store bulk drugs or dispense prescription drug orders.
D. A Class H pharmacy may only deliver filled prescriptions for dangerous drugs for the Class A pharmacy and may not deliver prescriptions for controlled substances.

Section Eight

Compounding Laws and Rules

Section Eight

Compounding Laws and Rules

See TFPDL Chapter H for complete rules with explanatory annotations.

I. **Nonsterile Compounding (TSBP Rule 291.131 or TFPDL pages H.5-18)**
   A. Establishes requirements for:
      1. Compounding of nonsterile preparations pursuant to a prescription or medication order for a patient from a practitioner in Class A (Community), Class C (Institutional), and Class E (Nonresident) pharmacies.
      2. Compounding, dispensing, and delivering of a reasonable quantity of a compounded nonsterile preparation in a Class A (Community), Class C (Institutional), and Class E (Nonresident) pharmacy to a practitioner's office for office use by the practitioner.
      3. Compounding and distribution of compounded nonsterile preparations by a Class A (Community) pharmacy for a Class C (Institutional) pharmacy.
      4. Compounding of nonsterile preparations by a Class C (Institutional) pharmacy and the distribution of the compounded preparations to other Class C (Institutional) pharmacies under common ownership.
   B. Nonsterile preparations may be compounded in anticipation of future prescription drug orders or medication orders based on routine, regularly observed prescribing patterns.
   C. Commercially available products may be compounded if they are not reasonably available from normal distribution channels in a timely manner, the pharmacy maintains documentation of this, and the prescribing practitioner has requested that the drug be compounded.
   D. A pharmacy cannot compound preparations that are essentially copies of commercially available products (e.g., slightly varying the strength) unless the prescribing practitioner specifically orders the strength or dosage form and specifies why the patient needs the product compounded.

E. A pharmacy may enter an agreement to compound and dispense for another pharmacy if the pharmacy complies with the centralized prescription dispensing rule. *(See TSBP Rule 291.123.)*
F. Pharmacists compounding nonsterile preparations must obtain continuing education appropriate for the type of compounding done by the pharmacist; inspect and approve all components, drug product containers, closures, labeling, and any other materials involved in the compounding process; review all compounding records for accuracy and conduct in-process and final checks to ensure that errors have not occurred in the compounding process; and be responsible for the proper maintenance, cleanliness, and use of all equipment used in the compounding process.
G. Compounding pharmacies must have a Class A prescription balance or analytical balance and weights which are subject to inspection by TSBP.
H. In addition to normal labeling requirements, a compounded prescription label must include the name(s) of the principal active ingredient(s) of the compounded preparation and a statement that the preparation has been compounded by the pharmacy.
I. All significant procedures performed in the compounding area shall be covered by written Standard Operating Procedures (SOPs) designed to ensure accountability, accuracy, quality, safety, and uniformity in the compounding process.
J. All compounding pharmacies must have a documented quality assurance and quality control program.
K. Office use compounding for distribution to physicians, Class C pharmacies, or veterinarians requires a written agreement with the practitioner or pharmacy. In addition, there are specific recordkeeping requirements, recall procedures, and products that must be labeled "For Institutional or Office Use Only – Not for Resale" or "Compounded Product" for distribution to veterinarians.

Note: The provisions for office use compounding in the Texas Pharmacy Act should be read in conjunction with the federal law on compounding including Sections 503A and 503B of the FDCA. There are concerns that the Texas law may be in conflict with the federal law.

L. Pharmacies may add flavoring to a prescription at the request of a patient provided certain conditions are met including having documentation that the flavoring does not alter clinical outcomes. This is not allowed for an OTC drug unless a prescription for the OTC drug is provided by a practitioner.
M. DEA generally allows pharmacists to compound narcotic controlled substances in Schedule II-V so long as the concentration of the final solution, compound, or mixture is not greater than 20%.

II. **Sterile Compounding (TSBP Rule 291.133 or TFPDL pages H.18-63)**
   A. General
      1. The Texas sterile compounding rule is similar to the requirements of USP Chapter <797>.
      2. Sterile preparations may be compounded pursuant to a prescription or medication order for a patient from a practitioner; in anticipation of prescription drug or medication orders based on routine, regularly observed prescribing patterns; as an incident to research, teaching, or chemical analysis and not for sale or dispensing; in reasonable quantities for a practitioner's office for office use by the practitioner; by a Class A-S pharmacy for a Class C-S pharmacy; and by a Class C-S pharmacy for distribution to other Class C or Class C-S pharmacies under common ownership.

      Note: The provisions for office use compounding in the Texas Pharmacy Act should be read in conjunction with the federal law on compounding including Sections 503A and 503B of the FDCA. There are concerns that the Texas law may be in conflict with the federal law.

      3. Sterile preparations may be compounded in anticipation of future prescription drug orders or medication orders based on routine, regularly observed prescribing patterns.
      4. Commercially available products may be compounded if a product is not reasonably available from normal distribution channels in a timely manner. In addition, the pharmacy must maintain documentation of the lack of availability of the product and that the prescribing practitioner has requested the drug be compounded.

5. A pharmacy cannot compound preparations that are essentially copies of commercially available products (e.g., slightly varying the strength) unless the prescribing practitioner specifically orders the strength or dosage form and specifies why the patient needs the product compounded.
6. A pharmacy may enter an agreement to compound and dispense for another pharmacy if the pharmacy complies with the centralized prescription dispensing rule.

B. Training Requirements
   1. All compounding personnel must receive didactic and experiential training that includes:
      a. Aseptic technique.
      b. Critical area contamination factors.
      c. Environmental monitoring.
      d. Facilities.
      e. Equipment and supplies.
      f. Sterile pharmaceutical calculations and terminology.
      g. Sterile pharmaceutical compounding documentation.
      h. Quality assurance procedures.
      i. Aseptic preparation procedures.
      j. Handling of cytotoxic and hazardous drugs, if applicable.
      k. General conduct in controlled area.
   2. Initial Training and Continuing Education.
      a. Pharmacists who compound sterile preparations or supervise personnel who compound sterile preparations must complete 20 hours of instruction through either a college of pharmacy or an ACPE approved course and complete on-the-job training at the pharmacy which cannot be transferred to another pharmacy unless the pharmacies are under common ownership.
      b. To renew a license, a pharmacist who engages in compounding sterile preparations shall complete 2 hours of CE related to compounding if engaged in compounding low- and medium-risk preparations or 4 hours if engaged in compounding high-risk preparations.
      c. Pharmacy technicians and pharmacy technician trainees who compound sterile preparations must complete 40 hours of instruction through either an ACPE approved course or a training program accredited by the American

Society for Health System Pharmacists and complete a structured on-the-job training program at the pharmacy which provides 40 hours of instruction and experience.
d. To renew a registration, a pharmacy technician who engages in sterile compounding shall complete 2 hours of CE related to compounding if engaged in compounding low- and medium-risk preparations or 4 hours if engaged in compounding high-risk preparations.

3. Evaluation and Testing.
   a. All personnel must be trained and pass media-fill tests for assessing aseptic technique.
   b. All compounding personnel shall successfully complete an initial competency evaluation and glove fingertip sampling procedure no fewer than three times before initially being allowed to compound sterile preparations for patient use. Sampling of compounding personnel glove fingertips shall be performed for all risk level compounding.
   c. Must be conducted during orientation and training, whenever the quality assurance program yields unacceptable results, and at least annually for low- or medium-risk products and twice a year for high-risk products.
   d. Media-filled tests.
      (1) Must be conducted at each pharmacy where an individual compounds low- and medium-risk sterile preparations. If pharmacies are under common ownership and control, the media-fill testing may be conducted at only one of the pharmacies provided each of the pharmacies is operated under equivalent policies and procedures and the testing is conducted under the most challenging or stressful conditions.
      (2) Media-fill tests must be conducted at each pharmacy where an individual compounds high-risk sterile preparations.
      (3) No preparation intended for patient use shall be compounded by an individual until the on-site media-fill tests indicate that the individual can competently perform aseptic procedures. An exception is a pharmacist may temporarily

compound sterile preparations and supervise pharmacy technicians compounding sterile preparations without media-fill tests provided the pharmacist completes the on-site media-fill tests within 7 days of commencing work at the pharmacy.

Must know all the classes.

C. Risk Levels for Sterile Compounding (USP Chapter 797)
   1. Low Risk.
      a. Compounded with aseptic manipulations entirely within ISO Class 5 or better conditions.
      b. Examples – Single transfers of sterile dosage forms from ampules, bottles, and vials using sterile syringes and needles, other administration devices, and other sterile containers; manually measuring no more than 3 manufactured products to compound drug admixtures and nutritional solutions.
      c. May be stored 48 hours at room temperature, 14 days if cold, or 45 days if frozen.
   2. Medium Risk.
      a. Multiple individual or small doses of sterile products are combined to prepare a product administered to multiple patients or one patient on multiple occasions; or involves complex aseptic manipulations other than single volume transfer; or requires unusually long compounding process.
      b. Examples – TPN fluids with multiple injections, detachments, and attachments of products to deliver to a final sterile container; filling reservoirs and infusion devices with multiple sterile products; and transfers of volumes from multiple ampules or vials into a single final sterile product.
      c. May be stored 30 hours at room temperature, 7 days if cold, or 45 days if frozen.
   3. High Risk.
      a. Nonsterile ingredients are used to prepare a sterile product; or sterile ingredients or devices or components are exposed to air quality inferior to ISO Class 5 for more than one hour; or nonsterile water-containing preparations are exposed more than 6 hours before being sterilized.

b. Example – Dissolving nonsterile bulk drug powders to make solutions which will be terminally sterilized.
  c. May be stored 24 hours at room temperature, 3 days if cold, or 45 days if frozen.

D. Environment
  1. Sterile preparations shall be compounded in a primary engineering control device which is capable of maintaining at least ISO Class 5 conditions. Primary engineering control devices include:
     a. Laminar Air Flow Hoods – Must be certified at least every 6 months.
     b. Biological Safety Cabinets – If being used for hazardous sterile products, they must be a Class II or III vertical cabinet and be located in an ISO Class 7 area. If being used for non-hazardous preparations, they must be located in a buffer area.
     c. Compounding Aseptic Isolators – Must be placed in an ISO Class 7 buffer area unless certain conditions are met.
     d. Compounding Aseptic Containment Isolator – If used for low- and medium-risk products, it must be placed in an ISO Class 7 buffer area unless specific conditions are met. If used for high-risk hazardous preparations, it must be placed in an area or room with at least ISO Class 8 conditions.
  2. Low- and Medium-Risk Compounding – Must have a clean room meeting specific requirements including having an ante and buffer area. *See TSBP Rule 291.133(d)(6)(A) or TFPDL pages H.38-39 for details.*
  3. High-Risk Compounding – In addition to the requirements for low- and medium-risk compounding, when high-risk preparations are compounded, the primary engineering device must be located in a buffer area that provides a physical separation through the use of walls, doors, and pass-throughs and has a minimum differential positive pressure of 0.02 to 0.05 inches water column.
  4. Cleaning and Disinfecting of Sterile Compounding Area. *See detailed requirements in TSBP Rule 291.133(d)(6)(F) or TFPDL pages H.41-43.*

5. Labeling of Sterile Prescription Drug or Medication Orders – In addition to labeling requirements for the class of pharmacy (A, B, C, or E), the label must contain:
    a. The generic or official name of the principal active ingredients.
    b. A beyond-use date determined as outlined in USP Chapter <797>.
    c. A statement for outpatient prescriptions (other than sterile radiopharmaceuticals) that the sterile preparation was compounded by the pharmacy.

E. Compounding Process
    1. All significant procedures shall be covered in written standard operating procedures (SOPs).
    2. Personnel Cleansing and Garbing. *See detailed requirements in TSBP Rule 291.133(d)(13)(C) or TFPDL pages H.50-52.*
    3. Quality assurance program must include media-fill test procedures, filter integrity testing, finished preparation release and checks, and environmental monitoring.
    4. Quality control program must include monitoring compounding environment and quality of compounded drug preparations including verification of compounding accuracy and sterility.

F. Immediate Use of Compounded Sterile Products – Provides an exemption from low-risk compounding requirements in an emergency or for immediate use where meeting the requirements would subject the patient to additional risk due to delay. Specific conditions must be met including that the preparation time does not exceed one hour and administration begins no later than one hour after compounding. Examples of immediate use of compounding sterile products are ERs, ICUs, etc.

G. Office use compounding and distribution to Class C pharmacies or veterinarians require a written agreement with the practitioner or pharmacy, specific recordkeeping requirements, recall procedures, and products that must be labeled, "For Institutional or Office Use Only – Not for Resale" or "Compounded Product" for distribution to veterinarians.

H. USP Chapter 800 – Handling Hazardous Drugs in Healthcare Settings

1. USP Chapter 800 details practice and quality standards for handling hazardous drugs in various healthcare settings from receipt, storage, compounding, dispensing, administration, and disposal.
2. It includes information on proper engineering controls and quality standards, personnel training, labeling, packaging, transport, and disposal of all hazardous drugs in various healthcare facilities.
3. The National Institute of Occupational Safety and Health (NIOSH) maintains a list of hazardous drugs and antineoplastic agents used in healthcare.
4. USP Chapter 800 becomes effective December 1, 2019. At the time of publication of this guide, the Texas State Board of Pharmacy had not adopted rules that would require pharmacies to comply with USP Chapter 800.

Section Nine

Practice Questions

Section Nine

Practice Questions

The following questions are designed to test your knowledge of the material in this review guide. The authors have no knowledge of specific questions on the Texas MPJE and have developed these questions independently. No representation is made that these questions are similar to actual questions on the MPJE. The Answer Key follows at the end of this section.

1. Dr. Trang calls your pharmacy and asks if she can call in a prescription for Vicodin for Mr. Garcia, a cancer patient who is well known to you. Dr. Trang states that Mr. Garcia cannot get relief from any other pain medication and that Mr. Garcia is unable to get to her office to pick up a prescription. She asks if you can fill the prescription and deliver it to Mr. Garcia's house. Which of the following is true?
   a. You cannot take a verbal prescription for Vicodin under these circumstances because Mr. Garcia is not a hospice patient.
   b. You can take the verbal prescription, but Dr. Trang must send you a written prescription for the Vicodin within 7 days.
   c. You can take the verbal prescription and fill the prescription, but it can only be for a 72-hour supply.
   d. Both b and c

2. Which of the following must be included as part of a prospective drug regimen review? **Select all that apply.**
   a. Drug-drug interactions
   b. Underutilization
   c. Rational drug therapy combinations
   d. Reasonable dose and route of administration

3. Pharmacist Ann is the owner and pharmacist-in-charge at City Drug, a busy community pharmacy in Waco, Texas. In a routine audit, Ann discovers a shortage of 500 dosage units of phentermine. Ann questions her pharmacy technician who admits to stealing the drugs. **Select all that apply.**
   a. If Ann determines that 500 dosage units is not a significant quantity, she does not have to report this to the DEA or TSBP.
   b. Ann must report this to TSBP but not DEA as phentermine is not a controlled substance under federal law.
   c. Ann must report this to DEA and TSBP.
   d. The initial report to DEA must be made within one business day.

4. A busy mother comes to your pharmacy to pick up a prescription for clobetasol cream 0.1% for her 12-year-old son. The prescription was electronically transmitted from Dr. Turner's office to your pharmacy earlier that day, was filled by another pharmacist, and is now ready for pick up. When the mother arrives, she informs you that the prescription was supposed to be for clobetasol lotion 0.1%, even though the prescription was written by Dr. Turner for clobetasol cream 0.1%. Which of the following is true?
   a. Because the prescription is for a child, you must call Dr. Turner to have the prescription changed from a cream to a lotion.
   b. Because the prescription was filled by another pharmacist, you must call Dr. Turner to have the prescription changed from a cream to a lotion.
   c. You can substitute the lotion for the cream and then send notification of the change to Dr. Turner.
   d. You must send the mother back to Dr. Turner to get a new written prescription for the lotion.

5. Who is authorized to witness the destruction of dispensed dangerous drugs by a consultant pharmacist at a nursing home? **Select all that apply.**
   a. An agent of the Texas State Board of Pharmacy
   b. A peace officer
   c. Another licensed pharmacist
   d. A registered pharmacy technician

6. Which of the following drugs may be prescribed by a DATA-waived practitioner for treatment of narcotic addiction? **Select all that apply.**
   a. Buprenorphine
   b. Naloxone
   c. Buprenorphine/Naloxone combination
   d. Methadone

7. When a pharmacy requests a transfer of a prescription from another pharmacy, the pharmacy where the prescription is held must complete the transfer
   a. In a timely manner
   b. Within 4 business hours
   c. Within 24 hours
   d. Within 48 hours

8. For which of the following prescriptions can a fax serve as the original prescription?
   a. A prescription for Demerol tablets for a 30-year-old post office worker
   b. A prescription for Ritalin tablets for a 12-year-old boy who lives with his parents
   c. A prescription for methamphetamine tablets for a 78-year-old LTCF patient
   d. A prescription for a morphine injection for an 86-year-old hospice patient
   e. Both c and d

9. All partial dispensings of Schedule II controlled substances for a nursing home patient must be completed within
   a. 72 hours
   b. 7 days
   c. 30 days
   d. 60 days

10. Pharmacist Fred believes that customers would like to buy small quantities of nonprescription drugs and decides to repackage bottles of 100 ibuprofen 200 mg tablets into amber prescription vials of 10 tablets and then sells them to the public. The vials are labeled with the name of the drug, the manufacturer, the lot number, and the expiration date from the original bottles. Which of the following statements are true? **Select all that apply.**
    a. Pharmacist Fred can repackage in this manner because it is for his own use in the pharmacy.
    b. Pharmacist Fred has misbranded the ibuprofen.
    c. The repackaging by Pharmacist Fred is considered compounding and within the practice of pharmacy.
    d. The repackaging by Pharmacist Fred is considered manufacturing.

11. On November 30, 2019, Dr. Williams asks you to prepare a customized medication package (Med Pak) for a patient to assist with the patient's compliance. The patient takes the following three drugs every morning: Losartan 25 mg, Synthroid 0.125 mcg, and Hydrochlorothiazide 25 mg. The stock bottles of the drugs to be used in the Med Pak have the following expiration dates: Losartan—December 2021; Synthroid – November 2020; Hydrochlorothiazide – June 2020. What should be listed as the beyond-use date for the Med Pak?
    a. November 30, 2020
    b. May 31, 2020
    c. June 30, 2020
    d. December 31, 2021

12. A pharmacist receives prescriptions for 12 different patients from the same physician over a 3-hour period. All of the prescriptions are written for patients from out of state and for the same combination of Vicodin, Xanax, and Soma. Which of the following are true? **Select all that apply.**
    a. If the pharmacist confirms that the physician has a valid license and DEA number, the prescriptions are likely valid and can be filled.
    b. If the pharmacist calls the physician and the physician confirms that he wrote the prescription and saw the patients, the prescriptions are likely valid and can be filled.
    c. The prescriptions are not likely to be valid because they appear to have not been issued for a legitimate medical purpose.
    d. If the pharmacist fills the prescriptions, he or she could be subject to disciplinary action by TSBP.

13. Which of the following is likely to be outside the scope of practice for a dentist to prescribe?
    a. Alprazolam
    b. Amoxicillin
    c. Oral contraceptives
    d. Lidocaine gel

14. Dr. Smith sets up a new private practice near your pharmacy. Soon after you begin to receive a number of prescriptions for methadone written by Dr. Smith. You call Dr. Smith and she explains to you that she is treating patients for opioid addiction. You should
    a. Document this conversation and continue to fill the methadone prescriptions.
    b. Ask Dr. Smith for her Drug Addiction Treatment Act (DATA) waiver identification code or "X" number and continue to fill the methadone prescriptions.
    c. Explain to Dr. Smith that she cannot prescribe methadone to treat opioid addiction and that you must refuse to fill any further prescriptions for methadone from Dr. Smith.
    d. Fill prescriptions for methadone 10 mg from Dr. Smith but refuse to fill prescriptions for methadone 40 mg.

15. On September 3, 2019, Dr. Garcia issues three prescriptions to Sally for Adderall. Each prescription is for a 30-day supply. The prescriptions are each written on separate official Texas prescription forms and all are dated September 3, 2019. Prescription #1 contains no additional instructions. On Prescription #2, Dr. Garcia writes "Do not fill before October 1, 2019." On prescription #3, Dr. Garcia writes "Do not fill before November 1, 2019." Which of the following is true?
    a. Dr. Garcia cannot postdate Schedule II controlled substance prescriptions in this manner; therefore, Prescription #2 and Prescription #3 are not valid.
    b. All the prescriptions are valid, but all must be dispensed by September 25, 2019.
    c. Prescription #1 is valid and must be dispensed by September 25, 2019. Prescription #2 is valid and must be dispensed by October 22, 2019. Prescription #3 is valid and must be dispensed by November 22, 2019.
    d. None of the prescriptions are valid because Adderall should not be written on an official Texas prescription form.

16. Which of the following products is required to be dispensed with the warning "Caution: Federal law prohibits the transfer of this drug to any person other than the patient for whom it was prescribed"?
    a. Buprenorphine
    b. Nalaxone
    c. Robitussin A-C with Codeine
    d. Lipitor
    e. All of the above

17. How many public members are appointed to the Texas State Board of Pharmacy?
    a. 1
    b. 2
    c. 3
    d. 5

18. A pharmacist received a bottle of generic tetracycline capsules from a wholesaler. The label stated that each capsule contained 500 mg of the drug, when it only contained 250 mg of the drug. There was nothing about the drug that would indicate to the pharmacist that this problem existed. The pharmacist dispensed several prescriptions before the problem was detected. Which of the following statements is true regarding the tetracycline?
    a. It is adulterated only.
    b. It is misbranded only.
    c. It is both adulterated and misbranded.
    d. It is neither adulterated nor misbranded but is instead a minor technical violation of the potency requirements.
    e. It is in violation of the Poison Prevention Packaging Act.

19. When ordering a Schedule II controlled substance from a supplier, how are the various copies of the federal order form distributed?
    a. Copy 1 and Copy 2 are sent to the supplier by the pharmacy at the time of the order. Copy 2 is returned to the pharmacy after the order is filled and is maintained at the pharmacy for a minimum of two (2) years.
    b. Copy 3 is sent to the supplier by the pharmacy with Copy 1 and Copy 2 maintained in the pharmacy. When the order is received, the pharmacy sends Copy 2 to DEA and maintains Copy 1 in the pharmacy for a minimum of two (2) years.
    c. Copy 1 and Copy 2 are sent to the supplier at the time of the order. Copy 3 is maintained at the pharmacy that placed the order, Copy 1 is maintained with the supplier, and the supplier forwards Copy 2 to DEA.
    d. Any of the above methods is permitted under the Federal Paperwork Reduction Act, as long as there is an audit trail to keep track of the whereabouts of controlled substances.
    e. None of the above

20. Pharmacist Vincent has some expired morphine tablets he would like to send to a reverse distributor for destruction. What documentation is required to accomplish this?
    a. DEA Form 41
    b. DEA Form 106
    c. DEA Form 222
    d. An invoice

21. A nonprescription bottle of 1¼ grain aspirin tablets cannot contain more than
    a. 24 tablets
    b. 36 tablets
    c. 50 tablets
    d. 100 tablets

22. Physician Assistant Nancy from Dallas, Texas calls in a prescription to your pharmacy for Billy, the 6-year-old son of Mrs. Davidson. The prescription is for a 30-day supply of phenobarbital with 5 refills. Which of the following is true?
    a. The prescription is not valid because a prescription for phenobarbital from a physician assistant is not valid.
    b. The prescription is not valid because a prescription from a physician assistant for a 6-year-old child is not valid.
    c. The prescription is valid, but only the original prescription and 2 refills may be filled. The remaining refills must be voided.
    d. The prescription is valid, and all the refills may be dispensed as long as they are dispensed within 6 months.

23. Which of the following is not part of the transaction data required to be maintained by a pharmacy when it purchases most prescription drugs from a wholesaler or manufacturer?
    a. Transaction Information
    b. Transaction History
    c. Transaction Statement
    d. Transaction Certification

24. Under the iPLEDGE Risk Evaluation and Mitigation Strategy (REMS) for isotretinoin, the maximum quantity that can be dispensed is a
    a. 7-day supply
    b. 14-day supply
    c. 30-day supply
    d. 60-day supply

25. The Texas State Board of Pharmacy is composed of
    a. 9 members consisting of 6 pharmacists and 3 public members
    b. 10 members consisting of 6 pharmacists, 1 pharmacy technician, and 3 public members
    c. 11 members consisting of 8 pharmacists and 3 public members
    d. 11 members consisting of 7 pharmacists, 1 pharmacy technician, and 3 public members

26. Before requesting reinstatement of a license which was revoked or lifting of a restriction on a license, a pharmacist must wait
    a. At least 6 months
    b. At least 12 months
    c. At least 2 years
    d. At least 5 years

27. Which of the following products requires a prescription to be dispensed?
    a. Humalog®
    b. Humulin N®
    c. Lantus®
    d. Both a and c

28. Secobarbital in suppository form is classified under what schedule?
    a. Schedule II
    b. Schedule III
    c. Schedule IV
    d. Schedule V

29. Which type of pharmacy may be in possession of prescription drug samples?
    a. A Freestanding Emergency Medical Care Center Pharmacy (Class F)
    b. A pharmacy owned by a charitable organization that is part of a healthcare entity providing care to indigent or low income patients at no or reduced cost
    c. A Central Prescription Drug Order Processing Pharmacy (Class G)
    d. A Community Pharmacy (Class A) if located in a medically underserved area

30. How often must a Class A pharmacy conduct an inventory of controlled substances?
    a. Every 6 months
    b. Annually
    c. Biennially
    d. A perpetual inventory is required that must be reconciled annually.

31. During each 2-year license renewal cycle to maintain certification to administer vaccinations and immunizations, a pharmacist must obtain how many hours of continuing education relating to disease states, drugs, and administration of immunizations or vaccines?
    a. 3 hours
    b. 6 hours
    c. 20 hours
    d. 30 hours

32. To renew a pharmacist license, a pharmacist who engages in compounding sterile preparations shall complete
    a. 8 hours of continuing education related to sterile compounding
    b. 4 hours of continuing education related to sterile compounding if compounding high-risk products
    c. 2 hours of continuing education related to sterile compounding if compounding low- or medium-risk products
    d. Both b and c

33. How can a prescriber prohibit generic substitution on a written prescription?
    a. By checking the "dispense as written" box
    b. By writing the words "dispense as written"
    c. By signing the prescription on the "dispense as written" signature line
    d. By writing the words "medically necessary" or "brand medically necessary"

34. Records of withdrawal of drugs when the pharmacy department is closed in a Class C pharmacy that employs a full-time pharmacist-in-charge must be reviewed by the pharmacist
    a. Within 24 hours
    b. Within 48 hours
    c. Within 72 hours
    d. Within 7 days

35. How many continuing education units (CEUs) are required to renew a pharmacist license?
    a. 20
    b. 2.0
    c. 30
    d. 3.0

36. Which of the following is not considered disciplinary action on a pharmacist's license?
    a. A reprimand
    b. A suspension
    c. A remedial plan
    d. A revocation

37. If a supplier cannot provide the entire quantity of a Schedule II controlled substance ordered on a DEA Form 222, the remaining quantity must be sent
    a. Within 72 hours
    b. Within 7 days
    c. Within 30 days
    d. Within 60 days
    e. None of the above

38. The Texas State Board of Pharmacy's policy regarding the filling or refilling of a prescription issued by a practitioner who subsequently dies is that a pharmacist
    a. May no longer fill such prescription under any circumstances
    b. May provide up to a 10-day supply and inform the patient to find a new practitioner
    c. May provide up to a 30-day supply and inform the patient to find a new practitioner
    d. May fill the initial prescription and all refills for up to one year

39. Which of the following is NOT a permissible use or disclosure of protected health information under HIPAA?
    a. Providing a list of all prescription medications to a patient's primary care physician
    b. Sending prescription information to a third-party insurance company for payment purposes
    c. Sending coupons for diapers to all pharmacy customers taking prenatal vitamins
    d. Providing a face-to-face recommendation of an OTC product to a patient based on the patient's symptoms and drug allergy profile

40. Which type of pharmacy may provide remote pharmacy services at a remote dispensing site through use of a Telepharmacy system?
    a. Class A pharmacy
    b. Class B pharmacy
    c. Class C pharmacy
    d. Class D pharmacy
    e. Class E pharmacy

41. For which of the following prescriptions may a pharmacist accelerate or advance refills?
    a. A prescription for a quantity of 30 Lipitor with 2 refills
    b. A prescription for a quantity of 30 Valium with 3 refills
    c. A prescription for a quantity of 30 tetracycline with 2 refills for a 16-year-old patient
    d. A prescription for a quantity of 30 tablets of Effexor for a 30-year-old patient

42. Which of the following products or prescriptions is exempt from the Poison Prevention Packaging Act's requirement for child-resistant containers?
    a. A prescription for 50 Nitro-Bid 6.5 mg capsules
    b. A prescription for 100 Isosorbide 10 mg sublingual tablets
    c. A prescription for 20 Erythromycin stearate 500 mg tablets
    d. Ibuprofen 200 mg tablets in a 30-count bottle

43. A mail-service pharmacy located in El Paso, Texas would obtain which type of pharmacy license?
    a. Class A
    b. Class C
    c. Class E
    d. Class F
    e. Class G

44. The pharmacist-in-charge of a pharmacy must have a policy and procedure to ensure that recalled drugs are removed from a pharmacy's inventory
    a. As soon as reasonably practical
    b. Within 24 hours
    c. Within 72 hours
    d. Within 7 days

45. Dr. Galloway writes a prescription for Percocet on July 7, 2019. What is the last day the prescription can be dispensed?
    a. July 14, 2019
    b. July 28, 2019
    c. January 7, 2020
    d. Technically there is no expiration date, but the pharmacist should use professional judgment.

46. For which class of recall is there a reasonable probability that the product could cause serious adverse effects or death?
    a. Class I
    b. Class II
    c. Class III
    d. Class IV

47. Which of the following are grounds for discipline of a pharmacist's license. **Select all that apply.**
    a. Refusing an inspection
    b. Failure to wear a lab coat while working
    c. Physically abusing a Board employee
    d. Failure to maintain required records

48. A nursing home patient who is prescribed estrogen must receive a copy of the patient package insert
    a. After one week of therapy
    b. Prior to the administration of the first dose and then every 30 days
    c. Annually
    d. If the doctor specifically requests it be given

49. When must a pharmacy electronically transmit the dispensing of a controlled substance prescription to the Texas State Board of Pharmacy?
    a. Immediately after the prescription was completely filled.
    b. No later than the next business day after the date the prescription was completely filled.
    c. No later than 7 days after the date the prescription was completely filled.
    d. No later than 21 days after the date the prescription was completely filled.

50. What is the maximum ratio of pharmacists to pharmacy technicians in a Class C pharmacy?
    a. 1:3 as long as 1 of the technicians is registered (only 2 can be trainees)
    b. 1:3 as long as 2 of the technicians are registered (only 1 can be a trainee)
    c. 1:4 as long as 1 of the technicians is registered (only 3 can be trainees)
    d. 1:4 as long as 2 of the technicians are registered (only 2 can be trainees)
    e. None of the above

51. A pharmacist receives a prescription for Fentanyl. The pharmacist consults with the prescriber of the medication. After such consultation, which of the following pieces of information may not be changed on the prescription even if the prescriber authorizes the change?
    a. Patient's address
    b. Patient's name
    c. Drug strength
    d. Drug quantity
    e. Directions for use

52. Which of the following are required elements of a pharmacy library in a Class A pharmacy? **Select all that apply.**
    a. Texas pharmacy laws and rules
    b. General drug information reference
    c. Pharmacotherapy: A Pathophysiologic Approach
    d. Basic antidote information and phone number of the nearest Poison Control Center

53. A DEA Form 41 is used to document
    a. Transfer of controlled substances to another registrant
    b. Transfer of controlled substances to a Narcotic Treatment Facility
    c. Loss or theft of controlled substances
    d. Destruction of controlled substances
    e. None of the above

54. Drugs dispensed for outpatient use in a Class F pharmacy may not exceed a
    a. 24-hour supply
    b. 48-hour supply
    c. 72-hour supply
    d. 7-day supply

55. In which location must a perpetual inventory be kept of all controlled substances?
    a. A Class A pharmacy
    b. A Class C pharmacy
    c. Any remote pharmacy location
    d. All of the above

56. The Texas Controlled Substance Prescription Monitoring program is administered by
    a. The Drug Enforcement Administration
    b. The Texas Department of Public Safety
    c. The Texas Department of State Health Services
    d. The Texas State Board of Pharmacy

57. Place the following in order from the least amount of time to the greatest amount of time.
   a. Time limit for filling a prescription for Xanax
   b. Time for a practitioner to deliver (or have postmarked) a written Texas Official Prescription after authorizing an emergency verbal prescription for Percocet.
   c. Days to provide the remaining quantity of a prescription for Ritalin that was partially filled (not for a LTCF patient)
   d. Number of days to provide notification to a patient's primary care physician that an immunization was provided in the pharmacy

58. An automated pharmacy dispensing system in a Class A pharmacy must be tested for accuracy at least
   a. Monthly
   b. Quarterly
   c. Every six months
   d. Annually

59. Anabolic steroids are classified under which schedule?
   a. Schedule II
   b. Schedule III
   c. Schedule IV
   d. Schedule V
   e. None of the above

60. Sterile preparations must be compounded in a primary engineering control device which is capable of maintaining at least
   a. ISO Class 3 conditions
   b. ISO Class 5 conditions
   c. ISO Class 7 conditions
   d. ISO Class 8 conditions

61. What must be provided prior to the first dose and every 30 days thereafter to a patient in an institutional setting who is taking an estrogen prescription?
   a. A safety data sheet
   b. A package insert
   c. A patient package insert
   d. A Medication Guide

62. Which inventory does not require the signature of the PIC to be notarized within 3 working days? **Select all that apply.**
    a. Change of ownership inventory
    b. Change of PIC inventory
    c. Initial inventory
    d. Annual inventory

63. Which of the following may not be on a Class D pharmacy's formulary even if it has been granted permission to have an expanded formulary?
    a. Amoxicillin
    b. Birth control pills
    c. Flexeril
    d. Cialis
    e. Both c and d

64. What is the maximum number of physicians a pharmacist may enter into a protocol to provide Drug Therapy Management services?
    a. No more than 3 physicians
    b. No more than 5 physicians
    c. No more than 7 physicians
    d. There is no maximum number

65. A physician issues a prescription for lidocaine in order to obtain a supply for the use in his office. What notation must the prescriber place on this prescription to make it a legitimate prescription that a pharmacist can fill?
    a. "Not for resale"
    b. "Own Use"
    c. "General Office Use Only"
    d. "Office Use"
    e. None of the above

66. A fire broke out in the front part of Debra's pharmacy, but the flames did not reach the prescription department. Can the drugs still be dispensed?
    a. Yes, as long as the containers are all closed.
    b. Yes, unless the drugs are heat sensitive.
    c. Yes, but only after notifying patients that their prescription may have been exposed to smoke.
    d. No, the smoke from the fire may have adulterated the drugs.

67. A prescription signed by a pharmacist practicing in a hospital, hospital-based clinic, or an academic healthcare institution working under delegated authority by a physician
    a. May be dispensed only if it is written for less than a 30-day supply
    b. May be dispensed if it is for a dangerous drug
    c. May only be dispensed at the outpatient pharmacy hospital, clinic, or academic healthcare institution
    d. Both b and c

68. Which of the following disciplinary actions taken against a pharmacist's license mean that a license is not in effect for a specified amount of time?
    a. Revocation
    b. Suspension
    c. Restriction
    d. Reprimand

69. What is the youngest age patient whom a pharmacist may provide a flu vaccine without a referral from a physician?
    a. Greater than age 7
    b. Greater than age 10
    c. Greater than age 14
    d. None of the above

70. A pharmacist compounding high-risk sterile products must pass media-fill tests at least
    a. Every month
    b. Every quarter
    c. Every six months
    d. Annually

71. Ms. Nguyen comes into the pharmacy to pick up her prescription while Pharmacist Marie is on a lunch break at Joe's Discount Pharmacy, but the prescription department is still open. The prescription was called in earlier in the day, and the prescription has already been filled and checked by Pharmacist Marie. The prescription is for methotrexate, and this is a drug that Ms. Nguyen has never taken before. Which of the following are true? **Select all that apply.**
    a. Pharmacist Marie must return from lunch break to counsel Ms. Nguyen.
    b. The prescription can be given to Ms. Nguyen by the pharmacy technician as long as written information regarding the drug is provided along with a notice that a pharmacist is available during normal business hours to answer any questions she may have.
    c. Pharmacist Marie cannot leave the facility for her lunch break.
    d. The prescription department cannot remain open while Pharmacist Marie is on a lunch break.

72. A pharmacist's continuing education records must be maintained
    a. For one year
    b. For two years
    c. For three years
    d. Until the next renewal cycle

73. Which of the following may a pharmacy technician NOT perform?
    a. Prescription data entry
    b. Placing the label on a prescription
    c. Transferring a prescription
    d. Bulk compounding
    e. None of the above

74. A pharmacy that plans to change location must notify TSBP at least how many days before the planned move?
    a. 10 days
    b. 14 days
    c. 30 days
    d. 60 days

75. A student intern designation expires if a student fails to take the NAPLEX/MPJE
    a. Within 3 months after graduation
    b. Within 6 months after graduation
    c. Within one year of graduation
    d. Within 18 months of graduation

Answer Key to Practice Questions

1. B
2. A, B, C, and D
3. C and D
4. C
5. A and B
6. A and C
7. B
8. E
9. D
10. B and D
11. C
12. C and D
13. C
14. C
15. C
16. A
17. C
18. C
19. C
20. C
21. B
22. C
23. D
24. C
25. D
26. B
27. D
28. B
29. B
30. B
31. A
32. D
33. D
34. C
35. D
36. C
37. D
38. C
39. C
40. A
41. A
42. B
43. A
44. B
45. B
46. A
47. A, C, and D
48. B
49. B
50. E

51. B
52. A, B, and D
53. D
54. C
55. C
56. D
57. C, B, D, and A
58. C
59. B
60. B
61. C
62. B and C
63. D
64. D
65. E
66. D
67. B
68. B
69. A
70. C
71. B and C
72. C
73. C
74. C
75. B